W9-CHR-509

MARY LYNN KELSCH has taught writing at the high school, college and university, and adult education levels. THOMAS KELSCH is the editor of *Foster's Daily Democrat,* a newspaper with a daily circulation of 20,000 readers. Both authors have had numerous articles published in newspapers and magazines.

Tom Kelsch

To
STAN *and* GRACE *and* BERT *and* LUCILLE
*whose knowledge and love of the power
and magic of words flowed into us well
before we could read.*

WRITING EFFECTIVELY:
A Practical Guide

MARY LYNN KELSCH
Lecturer, University of New Hampshire
Durham, New Hampshire

THOMAS KELSCH
Editor, Foster's Daily Democrat
Dover, New Hampshire

A SPECTRUM BOOK

PRENTICE-HALL, INC., *Englewood Cliffs, N.J. 07632*

Library of Congress Cataloging in Publication Data

Kelsch, Mary Lynn.
   Writing effectively.

   (A Spectrum Book)
   Bibliography: p.
   1. English language—Rhetoric. I. Kelsch, Thomas,
joint author. II. Title.
PE1408.K476   808'.042   80–22594
ISBN 0–13–969832–9
ISBN 0–13–969824–8 (pbk.)

© 1981 by Prentice-Hall, Inc., Englewood Cliffs, New Jersey 07632

A SPECTRUM BOOK

All right reserved.
No part of this book may be reproduced
in any form or by any means
without permission in writing from the publisher.

10 9 8 7 6 5 4 3 2 1

Printed in the United States of America

Prentice-Hall International, Inc., London
Prentice-Hall of Australia Pty. Limited, Sydney
Prentice-Hall of Canada, Ltd., Toronto
Prentice-Hall of India Private Limited, New Delhi
Prentice-Hall of Japan, Inc., Tokyo
Prentice-Hall of Southeast Asia Pte. Ltd., Singapore
Whitehall Books Limited, Wellington, New Zealand

Introduction

"Don't give me a person with ideas," the executive says. "Everyone has ideas. Give me the person who can express those ideas well."

It is one thing to have ideas. It is quite another to put them across to others so they take on meaning and substance. With all our modern conveniences—television, electronic games, computers that teach, home information banks—we also live in a world in which the art of communication is being lost. So many people are becoming passive receptacles. They receive information from others, usually through electronic means that require no effort. They are very inept at giving out information to others in any effective way.

Much has been said about the lost art of conversation. People don't talk anymore. Instead, they watch television together. They go to a movie, a sporting event, or an opera together. They play games together. At most, when they meet they talk about what they watched on television the previous night. "Did you see 'Mork and Mindy' last night? I liked the part where alien beings disguised as women were trying to torture him into revealing the secrets of earth and he thought they were trying to seduce him."

Those same people who have such trouble communicating are often people with very active minds. They have access to more information than any generation in history. Their facts may come from TV game shows, but their facts are accurate. They are better educated, have broader knowledge, have more exposure to oceans of information than any other people has ever dreamed of. In a typical day on television, you can take a French lesson, learn about the early Dutch still-life painters, study the sex life of sea horses, explore the African jungle or the plains of Jupiter, walk again in the court of Marie Antoinette, and watch what is happening around the world as it happens.

No other generation has been so knowledgeable, so full of ideas.

No other generation, however, has received the knowledge from such expert communicators. Communicating is becoming a professional occupation. Communication itself is a specialized body of knowledge, taught in college and improved through years of backwater experience. The ordinary person is not expected to communicate outside his circle. He is expected to receive communication, not give it.

He often lives up to what is expected of him. We have all experienced the frustration of knowing we have something to say but not being able to make people listen to it. We all feel there is so much more to us than we communicate. Because everyone is used to listening to newsmen, announcers, politicians, and other professional communicators, anyone who is less eloquent seems inadequate. We have all gotten into the habit of accepting information only from the professional communicators.

The professionals may say it better than we can. But then, they may not be saying what we want said. Worse yet, they may be convincing us that what they are saying is what we want said. "I never know what I think on any subject until I see the bumper sticker," says Erma Bombeck, a woman who expresses herself admirably. And forty million Americans say, "You know, that's exactly how I feel." If professionals do our communicating for us, they will also do our thinking for us. For thoughts without expression benefit nobody.

Somewhere in the mass of information we have been receiving we have needlessly buried our ability to give out information. We have actually reached the point where so few people communicate effectively that those who do are well rewarded, even in fields far removed from those associated with communication itself. There are fortunes to be made in all areas of human endeavor by those who can pass on to others what they discover.

That brings us full circle. When those who can communicate are valued, more people will learn to communicate.

All of us, having come through the American educational system, have had some training in expressing ourselves. We have the tools to do it. But we make errors in our efforts to communicate. Those errors—few in number—are measured against the efforts of the top of the field, the most polished and skillful communicators. Thus our attempts are found wanting. If we can't be Saul Bellow or Walter Cronkite, we won't try at all.

How much simpler and more beneficial it would be to correct our errors and learn to say things effectively! We don't have to reach the top. All we have to do is write clearly. If we can do that, we can benefit ourselves and others, no matter what our job or our position in life is or will be. And more and more our position in life can depend on our ability to do that. Like it or not, doors open to those who communicate effectively. Jobs open. Promotions open. High grades come more easily.

In this book, we are limiting ourselves to one basic and important area of communication: writing. Our thesis is that writing is easy. Anyone can do it. *You* can do it. If you cannot (or think you cannot), you are probably making a limited number of errors that are keeping you from being effective when you try to write what you are thinking. You are doing a few things wrong. You are paying a heavy price for not understanding a few fundamentals of effective writing. This book will try to eliminate those errors so that you can and will communicate effectively in this world where effective communication is such an asset.

To accomplish this, it must be understood that there is nothing magical about being a writer. It is not a vocation in which a limited number of eccentric geniuses are summoned by the Muses to perform mystical rites with pen and paper. There are no "chosen few" when it comes to writing. Writers are simply persons who write. Writers cover the full scale from poor to great. Average writers are fully as much writers as are geniuses.

If you write a lot, you learn some things about writing that you didn't know before and that other persons may not know. So you write better. If you work on your writing, study it, read about it, care about it, examine it, you can tap the knowledge garnered by previous writers about writing. This knowledge can improve your writing tremendously. Some of this knowledge is contained in this book.

The point is, writing is for everyone. Some skills require training. If you try to build bridges without training in engineering, you can expect disaster. Only a dentist knows how to fix teeth. You have to understand electronics to build a television set. Doctors have to be highly trained. Writers are not in the same league when it comes to training requirements. You don't have to be a highly trained professional to be effective.

To be a writer, all you have to do is sit down and write. To be a good writer, you have to know how to express yourself clearly and effectively. That is what we are trying with this book to help you do. But you don't need years of training and discipline. To write well, or to use writing effectively in furthering your career, whatever it is, you need only to be able to say effectively what you are thinking. That is a natural state, not the result of extensive training.

This book is for nonprofessional writers, for writers who wish to use writing for better grades, to relieve the frustration of not communicating well. It is for professionals in other fields who want to use writing as one of the tools available for doing their work better. It is also for people who would like to be published writers eventually, either as a vocation or as an avocation.

There is little here that will appeal to the established professional writer. There is little here that will appeal to the linguist or advanced communicator. We hope there are many things in this book that will help nonprofessionals write better.

The theory behind this book is one that we have had demonstrated to us over and over again. It is this: Those who have trouble writing are making a limited number of mistakes when they try to write. Most of these mistakes are easily corrected. Most of them occur because the writer does not understand what he should be doing.

In other words, in most cases there is no good reason why a person who does not write well cannot write well. He simply has to understand and correct the things that are keeping him from doing so. Over the years, we have collected and categorized some of the problems people have with writing. We have taken the most common, most crippling, and most easily corrected problems and collected them together in this book. We have added a few tips on how to eliminate them from one's writing. We feel anyone who eliminates the problems discussed in this book can and will be a good writer. We did not say just an acceptable writer. We mean anyone—you—can be a good effective writer. We feel if you are having trouble communicating in writing, you will benefit immensely from the tips in this book.

There are many, many people who think they cannot write. There is almost no one who can't write.

This little volume makes no pretense at being all-inclusive. Quite the contrary, it is intentionally selective. Likewise, the items are offered in no logical order. Instead we start with what we think the biggest problems are and work from there. There are many excellent books on the market that are extensive and inclusive. There are many that follow the writing process every step of the way from beginning to end. We will include a bibliography so that if you want to know more you will know where to find it. There is much important material about writing that you will not find here. We encourage you to move from this book to weightier works and deeper discussions on the subject.

What you will find here, though, is a small collection of the problems you are most likely to have with your writing. We hope what we have to say about them will help you write better. You may not be making some of the mistakes we talk about. We are willing to bet, however, that if you are having trouble expressing yourself effectively in writing, you are making some of these mistakes, maybe many of them. They are hurting your writing and you unnecessarily.

If some of the tips in this book help you write better, we will be more than satisfied. If the tips encourage you to write more, we will be happy. If they help you acquire the pleasure and satisfaction we find in words and their skillful use in communication, if after you have used this book you *enjoy* writing, we will be overjoyed.

Contents

CHAPTER ONE

The Controlling Idea

A traveler can get lost for two reasons. He does not know where he is going, or he does not know how to get there.

Writers get lost for the same two reasons. However, while no sensible traveler would think of starting out until he knew where he wanted to end up, writers do so regularly.

Such ill-advised literary journeys lead to a basic misunderstanding about writing. So many people who would like to write effectively think they don't know how. They struggle and strive, putting maximum effort into trying to polish their writing into something acceptable and understandable. They become frustrated with their efforts, weary of the struggle, and eventually decide they simply cannot write, they have no talent for it. So they give up.

Unfortunately, far too often the writing itself is not the problem. The trouble often is centered in their confusion as to where they want to go, what they want to say, rather than in their inability to grasp the means of getting there.

Writers who don't know where they are going or what they are trying to say will naturally get lost and discouraged. They will wander aimlessly through the byways and thickets

1

until sooner or later they will give up trying to write well. They quit because they do not understand the nature of their problem.

Fortunately, this problem, which haunts so many people who would like to write but think they are not good at it, is a solvable one. In fact, it is a fairly easy one to solve. It is a matter of potential writers becoming aware of the error they are making, the specific error of not sorting out thoroughly what they want to say before they try to say it. Writers, like travelers, must first decide where they want to go. Where they are going then becomes a beacon, a guiding star. As long as they keep their eyes firmly fixed on that star, they are not going to get lost. The road may even turn out to be smooth and pleasant.

That guiding star in writing is called a controlling idea. Our first three chapters will be devoted to learning to formulate and use a controlling idea. Only after the controlling idea is guiding our writing will we tackle the specifics of how to say something well.

Definition of a controlling idea

What exactly is a controlling idea? A controlling idea is a brief statement of what the finished work will be and what it will try to accomplish. Simple? Yes. But what a difference it makes in writing!

Even the most common and elementary writing should have a controlling idea. You are writing home to your parents from college. Your controlling idea may be to tell them what is happening to you, to explain your class schedule, to give them the flavor of your life in the dorm, to ask them for money, or some such. The controlling idea will dictate what you put in the letter and what you leave out. If your controlling idea is to con them out of some bills, you probably will not spend much time describing the kid who wants to take you to New Orleans for Mardi Gras. Nor will you dwell on the excellent dorm food or the free laundry in the basement. You will concentrate, perhaps, on the pressure of studies and the need for outlets and relaxation, or the price of reference books.

Or maybe you are a teacher and the principal wants to know why there was so much noise coming from your classroom yesterday. Your memo to him is no place to talk about the staff Easter party, to mention what inflation is doing to your salary, or to explain the new textbook you came across last week. It might be the place to mention the value of discussions in learning, the energy youth exhibit in the spring, and the fact that scholarship and silence are not synonyms.

Qualities of a good controlling idea

In this chapter we are going to look at controlling ideas from a number of points of view, examining them, checking their qualities, reviewing how others employ them, in short, thoroughly familiarizing ourselves with them. Later chapters will take up how to decide on a controlling idea and how to develop it into a written work.

Not every idea that pops into your mind is a fit subject for a piece of writing. Not every idea is a controlling one. The controlling idea has certain distinctive qualities, three of them, that make it capable of guiding your mind and your pen effectively.

Importance

To begin with, the idea must be important. It must be important enough to sustain the work, that is, to make the writing worth reading. What is important enough for that?

Anything that is original, illuminating, or interesting. But it should be at least one of the three. By original, we mean anything that is likely to be unknown to your readers. By illuminating, we mean anything that contributes to the understanding your reader will have of a subject. By interesting, we mean anything your reader will want to know.

Keep an eye on the intended reader in deciding if a subject is important enough to be a controlling idea for you. Your parents are probably interested in everything that happens to you. Thus a letter to them can be gossipy and concerned with trifles. If you are writing a composition for English class, the teacher will give you subjects or guidelines on picking subjects. A short cut to auditing billing may be of very limited interest to the general reader, but if it will improve efficiency and increase profit for your company, your boss is going to find it most interesting. In a memo to your boss, it is a great controlling idea. It is original, illuminating, AND interesting. To the general public, forget it. If you are trying to sell a novel to a publisher, the controlling idea had better be a theme of substance and interest, and its proposed development must be of some originality. If you are submitting a doctoral dissertation, the controlling idea had better be of value to the discipline in which you are specializing.

Limitation

The controlling idea must also be limited enough to make the writing task reasonable and manageable. Ah, there's the rub. Poor writers usually try to keep their subjects too broad. They try to say everything about a general category. They end up saying nothing. Television programming is an important and interesting topic. It is not a controlling idea, though, because it is too broad. It is a topic, a subject. A controlling idea is an idea about a topic. A controlling idea on the topic of television programming might be: The Muppets are popular because they mirror the human condition; or, Walter Cronkite has more influence on the thinking of Americans than Jesus Christ; or, Sports programs are creating a passive, spectator mentality toward life.

In other words, a category is not a controlling idea; neither is a generality, a topic, or a subject. Take that important category and limit it to something manageable. The favorite first composition topic of teachers, "How I Spent My Summer Vacation," is not a controlling idea. It is a category. It gives you an area in which to search for a controlling idea. A controlling idea in that area, the guiding light to a composition about your summer vacation, could be: "I finally got to know my horse well and I found him to be a good friend." or: "Do you know what happens when you put shaving cream in your camp counselor's toothpaste tube? He really foams at the mouth." or: "Working on a road construction crew is one way to stay in shape for football."

There is a quick way to test a controlling idea's validity: Make sure your controlling idea is a sentence. Giving the subject a verb and an object is a good way to limit it properly.

Clarity

There is one more quality an important and limited controlling idea must have. It must be clear—in the mind of the writer first and above all, so that it can come through clearly to the reader. The writer must have thoroughly sorted out in his head what his idea is. He must have discarded all the other attractive and distracting ideas that pull at him.

If the writer knows clearly what he wants to say, he may or may not be able to convey the idea to the reader. But if his controlling idea is less than clear to him, he definitely will not be able to. He has no chance. His writing will not accomplish what it should or could. We cannot even say it will not accomplish what it set out to, because without a clear controlling idea the writer does not set out to accomplish anything in particular.

Importance, limitation, clarity. These qualities of a good controlling idea do not generally appear in final, workable form immediately. Usually, the mind must work its way to them. The gap between "I have an idea," and "I have a good controlling idea" is wide. Until it is crossed, though, writing is, literally, pointless. How you bridge that gap is the subject of Chapter Two. For now, let us look more deeply into the nature of a controlling idea by analyzing what it does.

Function of a controlling idea

Why is it that the controlling idea is such a beacon before the eyes of a writer? For four reasons, all of which we have touched on already, but which are worth mentioning individually to help understand how a controlling idea functions and how one can be made to work for you.

Guiding the development

The first change in your writing when you start thinking in terms of a controlling idea is that you and your writing have a definite purpose. Every word you write must work toward that purpose. Not only the supporting ideas, but the very wording of those ideas is dictated for you by the controlling idea.

What is wrong with this passage?

"Through the windy night, John moved toward the distant light. Tall and handsome, he walked slowly but relentlessly. That lighted window marked the safety and comfort of home. He wanted to run, but he knew stumps, branches, and a shallow stream, crouched between him and the light, waiting to trip him, waiting to ruin his shoes, waiting to turn his homecoming from a loving reception into a scolding. So he forced himself to proceed carefully, measuring every step."

Once you know that the controlling idea is: "John walked home cautiously because he did not want to ruin his reception," it is easy to pick out the one phrase that does not contribute to the story. "Tall and handsome" adds nothing. It confuses the reader since the rest of the story points to a smaller boy. It does not fit the controlling idea. It may be true, but the story is stronger for its omission.

Dictating the content

Beyond giving the writer his purpose, the controlling idea also completely dictates the content of the writing. Everything in the composition assumes its importance and position by its relationship to the controlling idea. We will go into this point in more detail later, when we discuss organization and development of the controlling idea into a written work. For now, suffice it to emphasize that the controlling idea provides the key by which all the pieces of a composition are fitted together into a meaningful whole. If the controlling idea is a proposition to be proven, the arguments can all be lined up in order of importance. Illustrations and examples can be sorted out according to the contribution they make to the proof of the controlling idea and according to the supporting arguments they best illustrate.

For instance, consider this controlling idea: Medicare is a necessity in our inflation-prone society.

After some thought, you might come up with the following reasons to support the controlling idea:

1. Inflation takes away the ability of persons on fixed incomes to meet spiraling medical bills.

2. Old people tend to get sick more often.

3. Your aunt died at home of a blood clot because she could not afford to enter a nursing home.

4. Doctors don't make house calls anymore.

5. With the breakdown of family ties in our mobile society, the aged cannot depend on their children for support.

6. There is no medical cure for the isolation and loneliness of the aged.

7. Hospital costs have risen more than 300 percent in the past five years.

By keeping your eye firmly fixed on proving your controlling idea, you will have little difficulty deciding that statement one is the most important. Number five is second, number two is third. Number three and number seven are examples under number one; and statements four and six, while probably true and important, are not directly related to your controlling idea and should be deleted.

Your controlling idea, then, has made it easy to line up your supporting arguments in order of importance. Your outline would look like this:

I. Medicare is a necessity in our inflation-prone society.
   A. Inflation tends to take away the ability of persons on fixed incomes to meet medical bills.
      1. Hospital costs have risen more than 300 percent in the past five years.
      2. An aunt died at home of a blood clot because she could not afford to enter a nursing home.
   B. With the breakdown of family ties in our mobile society, the aged cannot depend on their children for support.
   C. Old people tend to need more medical aid because they tend to get sick more often.

From such an outline, you could build an effective piece of argumentative writing. It is strong because the controlling idea is clear and every supporting point is geared to establishing the controlling idea effectively.

Dictating the style

The controlling idea also dictates the style. Some kinds of writing are completely inappropriate for the expression of some ideas. Obviously, a scholarly approach to throwing garbage into a truck is as unlikely to be effective as a humorous style of relating an accident that killed a busload of school children.

More common than such major improprieties are the thousands of nuances in style that can be adjusted to the needs of the controlling idea. A Paul Bunyan tale will be written in a completely different style from a John Steinbeck story. A Bill Cosby comedy routine is nothing like a Bob Hope routine. Their styles are different. They start with different controlling ideas on how to make people laugh. Anyone can spot the differences between the high-powered style of Ian Fleming's James Bond stories and the disenchanted spy style of John LeCarré. Their controlling ideas are different. They are both writing spy stories, but they are trying to accomplish widely different objectives.

It all depends on what you are trying to accomplish. In other words, it all depends on the controlling idea.

You are a secretary. Your boss has asked you to attend a meeting he cannot and to give him a summary of what was said. You write:

"Phillips gave the principal speech. He was concerned about the amount of waste being generated by faulty workmanship on the assembly line. He pointed out that of 10,000 units produced last month, 1,500 (15 percent) had been rejected for flaws. Ten years ago less than 5 percent of the units had had to be rejected. With the 20 percent profit margin we use, he said the rejections were bringing us unacceptably close to losing money. He did not offer any solutions, but asked that all managers and foremen be prepared to discuss wastage at the meeting next month. Mr. Henson from production was the only other person to say anything important. He claimed that the workmanship had not declined. He said monitoring was stricter and regulations were tougher. He said units now rejected would never have been stopped ten years ago. He also said government regulations had slowed the assembly lines."

Now you are writing to a girlfriend about having attended a managers' meeting for your boss. Now you write:

"Remember old Phillips, the cantankerous district manager who can't hold his secretaries and had the suit filed against him by Joannie for making a pass at her? Well, he carried on for almost an hour about faulty workmanship. He said 15 percent of the units had to be rejected last month. I'm surprised it wasn't more, what with the new union negotiations under way and the determination of management to keep costs down by diluting the raw materials. He talked about low profit margins, but did not account for the fact that stockholders got large dividends last quarter. I was so mad, especially when he did not have any answer. In typical style, he told the others to have some answers ready next meeting. Mark Henson, the young foreman with the broad shoulders I was telling you about, finally put him in his place. He said quality was better than ever, it was just that standards were stricter. He also said it wasn't their fault the line was slower. Government regulations had caused that. Phillips was fit to be tied when the meeting broke up."

The controlling idea dictates the style.

We will return to a more complete discussion of style in Chapter Seven. For now, one word of caution. Don't force style. Let it flow naturally from the controlling idea. Nothing sounds more pompous than a style that does not ring true. If the controlling idea does not seem to dictate any specific style, keep your writing natural and unadorned. You will be surprised how many nuances will flow from what you are trying to accomplish, that is, from your controlling idea.

Keeping the writer to the point

The final important task the controlling idea performs is that of keeping the writer to the point. Only what promotes the controlling idea can be included in any work. One of the biggest problems of most occasional writers is that of excluding everything that does not belong. They have worded something extremely cleverly, or they know some interesting fact. They simply cannot bring themselves to exclude those gems they know the world is waiting to hear. At times they even make elaborate efforts to set the stage perfectly so they can bring these marvelous statements in with maximum impact.

Unfortunately, even a brilliant paragraph can ruin a work if it does not belong. And those little masterpieces, not the dull, routine statements, are the most difficult to leave out.

If you keep your eye on the controlling idea, the problem is obvious in the following passage. If you don't, you would never think of blaming the brightest sentence in the paragraph.

"Unlike many of the big boomers on the professional golf tour today, Chi Chi Rodriguez depends upon accuracy and finesse. His drives would open eyes in any country club setting, and they are indeed remarkable for his slight build. But on the tour, he is constantly playing from slightly farther away, using one extra club length, pitching when others are putting. He expresses nothing but gracious admiration for the longer-hitting giants. For instance, referring to Jack Nicklaus' many business interests yet evident golfing superiority, he remarked,

'Nicklaus is a legend in his spare time.' Still, Chi Chi has to put out that little extra, swing a little harder, concentrate a little more, to keep up. It is a credit to his spirit and competitive drive as well as to his singular abilities that he managed to remain a top golfer for so many years despite his tiny frame."

Chi Chi's remark about Nicklaus was clever and is worth repeating. It really is not pertinent to this passage, however. It does not specifically refer to Nicklaus' driving ability, and, despite the maneuvering by the writer before and after the statement to make it fit, it distracts from the passage. Remove that clever but forced sentence and see how much smoother and clearer the passage is.

Expressing the controlling idea in the writing

The controlling idea is a tool for the writer. We strongly recommend, especially if you are not completely familiar with the writing process, that you physically write out the controlling idea. Put it on the desk in front of you as you write, and don't lose sight of it, not even for one word.

In your composition, though, the controlling idea can be expressed in varying degrees and in different ways, depending on what you are trying to accomplish. The controlling idea need not be part of the text. It is for your good and for the good of the writing that you work it out clearly. Its actual appearance in the text is incidental.

Stating the idea at the beginning

Some kinds of writing routinely state the controlling idea plainly at the beginning. Debating, argumentative writing, many essays use this method. Business writing almost never leans on an indirect approach. It comes right to the point. Stating the controlling idea immediately is also common in journalism. The famous and overworked "who, what, when, where, and how" of newspaper lore is a variation on the immediate statement of the controlling idea.

"After three years of debate and countless hours of argument, only the governor's signature separates the right-to-know bill from becoming law. The State Senate voted yesterday by a narrow margin to pass the controversial measure."

"If you could ask the president of the United Stated one question, what would it be? That's the dilemma some 1,000 residents are facing as they prepare to meet the president at a special town meeting this evening."

"Memo to Mr. Bailey, vice president.
Re: More efficient use of metal shavings.
Every day, this plant throws out two tons of metal shavings from the production line. The shavings cannot be used for making our normal products because recycling them would weaken their tensile strength. There are many products they could be used for, however. Couldn't we set up a subsidiary assembly line, melt the shavings back down, then mold them into a product not requiring high tensile strength? We could increase our profits by as much as $100,000 annually by doing so. Here is a list of some products we could make with the shavings."

Building up to the controlling
idea

Leading off with the controlling idea is not always the best policy, however. If suspense, or building to a climax, is essential to the writing, you will destroy the effect by giving away immediately where you are going. Be patient. Be subtle.

Let the controlling idea unfold. Let it grow on the reader, become more and more clear as the work progresses. Most works of fiction, most narrations (for example, story telling) reveal their controlling idea slowly. Much good argumentative writing and many essays also effectively build to a climax.

"John swung wildly at the sound. His arms found only air. Mocking laughter rang out behind him. He turned to face his tormentor, determination creasing his brow. He stalked him slowly, carefully. A log reached up and tripped him. He sprawled forward, cutting his hand on a stone as he broke his fall. The laughter again. His face in the mud, he cursed the Creator who had decreed he be born blind."

"It's simple, it's cheap and it's effective."

The gradual revelation of the controlling idea is the substance of suspense stories. The reader does not know the significance of the half-empty decanter or of the music box that plays in the night. If he did, the writing would lose its force and its interest. It would not be effective.

The same reasoning applies to the use of the gradual revelation of the controlling idea in argumentative writing. Writing that builds from the weakest argument to the strongest, ending with a fully developed controlling idea, is often the most effective. We will take up more completely in Chapter Three how to use arrangement of supporting ideas most effectively in writing.

Not stating the controlling idea

As we said before, the controlling idea need not be expressed in a piece of writing at all. Perhaps in most cases it is not. The purpose of the controlling idea is to guide the writer to effectiveness. Many plays, poems, novels, and allegories never state the controlling idea. The same procedure works equally well in most forms of writing. If employed properly, the writing will still send the message to the reader. The important thing is that the writer have the guiding star and use it to reach his destination without getting lost. Expression of the controlling idea in the writing has little in itself to do with the success of the work.

What has everything to do with the success of the work is the existence of that controlling idea in the mind of the writer.

Summary

The controlling idea, then, is a writer's tool. It is a guiding star or road map the writer uses to make sure his writing accomplishes what he wants it to. It is a tool good writers are not too proud to use routinely, yet one that poor writers constantly try to do without. It may not be a part of the work, but it is the dominating force that dictates the work. Failure to use a controlling idea is one major cause of frustration and confusion in many writers who could be much more effective.

A topic or subject, however, is not a controlling idea. To become a controlling idea, a topic or subject must be important, limited, and clear.

Try using controlling ideas whenever you write. You'll like the results. So will your readers, your teachers, your bosses, and—maybe eventually—your editors.

CHAPTER TWO

Finding
A Controlling Idea

There is a difference between knowing what a controlling idea is and picking a controlling idea to guide you through a piece of writing.

A quarterback has many options when it comes to calling the next play. Only a few will lead to a touchdown. He has to pick one. The one he picks becomes the controlling idea for the whole team. Each member of that team then tries to make his individual contribution to the success of the play.

The writer is the quarterback. He has thousands, millions, of options open to him. But he must select only one. The idea he selects first of all must be one that has a chance of success. It must be a play that will work. Secondly, the writer must marshal all the surrounding ideas in such a way that each does its task perfectly. If these two conditions are present—if the idea is a good one and the supporting material is made to do its job—the writing will succeed.

In this chapter, we will tackle the problem of picking a controlling idea that will succeed.

The question, then, is: How do you pick a controlling idea? How do you set about finding an appropriate one? And how do you limit it to a well-chosen sentence?

The first thing to realize is that controlling ideas almost always have to be refined and defined and redefined. Very few appear in their final, successful form immediately. Ideas come forward readily; controlling ideas are much more bashful.

We have found that writers use three different methods of choosing and isolating controlling ideas. The first way is the easiest. It applies to those lucky times when you know before you start what you are going to write. In other words, the first way is to have the controlling idea clear in your mind before you write.

The second way is the classic and traditional way, taught in English and writing courses from way back. Pick a topic and reduce it to a controlling idea through restriction.

The third way is probably the most common. Pick a topic (rather than a controlling idea) and try to write a paper on it. Then, having made that effort, analyze what you are saying; work out from what you have written what your controlling idea is. Then rewrite to fit that idea.

The natural way for writers seems to be the third way. It also generally leads to the very troubles we are trying to avoid. Since it is so common, though, it seems to us to make more sense to learn to harness that method than to demand that writers give it up entirely and force themselves to use one of the other methods. So in the third way we will be dealing with ways of converting thoughtless starts into effective controlling ideas.

Start with something to say

Obviously, there will be many times that you will be writing with a specific idea in mind. You will have something you want to say or something you must say. In many ways, this is the easiest kind of writing because you start with the controlling idea already born. Half the battle is over before you start. The coach has sent in the play from the sidelines. You know where you want to go. You want to tell your boss about a new procedure to speed up production and cut costs. You are entering a contest on the topic: Why I like Puffy-Puffy Polyurethane Pillows. You want to tell your sister who lives in Georgia that you are engaged. You were making a deposit when armed robbers came in and you were taken hostage, now a magazine wants to know what it was like. You have this great idea for a novel based on your love life. You have made a DNA discovery that will provide a vaccine for cancer. Since the teacher assigned you to write on what you did during your vacation, you can't wait to tell about your trip to Europe.

These are glorious moments for a writer. If you have experienced them, you know such writing can be simple. That writing is so simple when you have the right controlling idea is to us the most solid proof possible of the importance of formulating the controlling idea before you write. ANYONE can write when he knows what he wants to say. We are trying to get you to know every time before you start to write.

Unfortunately, when you think you already know your controlling idea, your mind and your enthusiasm could be laying a trap for you. The writing could turn out to be far more complicated than you imagined. You may find words gushing out in all directions. You may find you cannot say all you wanted to say, or you may have trouble deciding what to take up first.

Beware. You may be doing exactly what we are trying to persuade you not to do. You may, despite happy appearances to the contrary, be writing without a good controlling idea, without really knowing what play you have called.

What happened? It all seemed so clear when you started. You could not have been more sure that you did indeed have a brilliant controlling idea. This is the weakness of the preordained controlling idea. It often is not one.

Let us look a little more closely at some of the problems that could have led you astray. In so doing, we will be considering some of the most common dangers, most common pitfalls, of the spontaneous controlling idea.

Too broad a topic

The most probable pitfall of the spontaneous controlling idea is that the thought is too broad. What seems to be a controlling idea is probably a topic. There are too many ways in which you can proceed. Before you started, did you bother to write out your controlling idea? Are you able to put into one brief statement what your writing is going to accomplish? Or are you so sure nothing can go wrong that you just happen to skip that step? Even if you are sure you have a good spontaneous controlling idea, write it out. Test it. If you do have a controlling idea, it will cost you about thirty seconds to state it. If you do not have one, the time saved will be lost one hundredfold farther down the trail.

Being taken hostage by bank robbers can be described in many different ways. So can a vacation in Europe. Both are topics. They only look like controlling ideas. What, then, might be a genuine controlling idea about being taken hostage? Something that is limited enough to give you and your pen direction. When he first pointed that gun in my direction and said, "You. Come with me," terror blotted out everything else; but as time went on, I found my mind plotting ways to subvert him and aid my escape. With that controlling idea, you could concentrate on your feelings and you could pick illustrations that portrayed your progression from terror to plotting.

The problem with the vacation topic is to avoid turning it into a directionless travelogue. ". . . then we did this, after which we went here, followed by a day in that city, after which we did this again." A simple narrative, linear account of your trip to Europe might get you by, but it more likely would not satisfy either you or your teacher. More likely, you would feel the need to comment on your experiences. And once you started doing that, you would be destroying the controlling idea behind the strict narrative. You would begin to ramble. So do not even start with a controlling idea so weak you know you cannot stick to the path. Rather, how about picking an overwhelming impression left with you by your trip? Explain and prove it by a sampling of events you experienced that illustrate it. Something like: Nobody can see Europe in fourteen days; everything becomes a blur. Or: The trains in Europe not only link countries and cities, they also provide passengers that reveal more about an area than a month of study could yield. Or: The hostility of Europeans toward the American tourist was not borne out by my stay in France.

Illustrations are seldom ideas

The second problem with spontaneous controlling ideas is that what looked like a controlling idea may actually only be an illustration or story. A good story has a point. That point is more likely to be the controlling idea than the story itself. If you do not grasp the point of the story as the controlling idea, the story will probably be directionless and punchless. A story makes a good example and can be an effective illustration. It seldom is the controlling idea.

On your way to the supermarket, you witnessed an accident. You want to tell that story and you feel it is a good controlling idea. But is it? Does it have a point, or is it simply a linear narrative? What really struck you may not have been the accident itself. It may have been the pain the victims were experiencing, the reckless driving that caused it, the cool efficiency of the police, or the strange instrument the firemen used to pry open the cars. Such impressions would make much better controlling ideas. Again, they give a point and direction to your writing. They are what you really want to say.

Idea may not be clear

The chances of a controlling idea being synonymous with the topic you want to write about are not that great. It is dangerous to think you have a controlling idea just because you know what you want to write about. Topics seem so clear. But having a clear topic is so different from having a clear idea of what you want to say about that topic. The gap is bridged only after you see the problem. And the most practical way to see the problem is the simple one of writing out what you think your controlling idea is. We cannot emphasize too much the importance of expressing the controlling idea in a sentence. It not only guides you later in deciding how to order your paper—what is pertinent and what is irrelevant, etc.— it also sheds so much light on the strengths and weaknesses of the idea. Verbalizing clarifies. It is so easy to think you know what you want to say. So state it in one sentence. That is the way to find out if you are indeed following a guiding star to your destination or if you are instead chasing a firefly that is constantly changing direction and constantly blinking off.

Choose a topic and limit it

There is a logical way to approach controlling ideas and the formulation of them. It is the way universally taught in older textbooks on writing. It is a multistep process involving choosing a topic, limiting it, gathering material, reworking the topic, and so on until it is a clear and effective controlling idea.

It is a dry, scholarly process. It is not much fun. It demands discipline and effort. It has only one saving grace: It works. It works well. It has worked for many, many excellent writers and for many beginners who have learned to use it. It is the one method that can almost guarantee results, even when you do not know the topic well or when you do not feel like writing but must.

Unfortunately, many writers think of themselves as artists, as creative free spirits who cannot be governed by the disciplines of mere mortals while they sit around and wait for the Muses to inspire.

Nonsense. Logic and discipline do not stifle the creative instincts. They give them form and brilliance. People who write regularly and successfully always eventually face the problem of trying to produce on command, at a time they do not feel like it, or on a topic they do not enjoy. And they find themselves forced to take this traditional approach to developing a controlling idea. They do it because this method succeeds. If followed faithfully, this method can and will lead you to a good controlling idea. But it will be work, not pleasure.

In fact, the other two methods described in this chapter are merely more glamorous sons of this stodgy father. They are popular, acceptable, even exciting ways of disguising a basic thought process for reaching a controlling idea. That thought process is laid out plainly in this method.

Selecting a controlling idea is basically a six-step process of refinement of a general topic.

Pick a topic

First, you pick a topic. As we have been stressing, that is not the same as picking a controlling idea. Sometimes the topic will be assigned to you by either your teacher or your editor. At other times you will have an idea of your own that you want to write about. And sometimes you will have to scour your mind until you come up with an acceptable topic.

In the last case, the simplest way is to select a subject or event you are interested in. Swimming. Animals. Travel. Archaeology. Political conventions. Football. Television. The man sitting next to you. Find a topic you want to and could write about. That is all there is to the first step.

Limit the topic

The second step in this process is the key one. Limit the topic you have picked. This is where a topic undergoes transformation into a controlling idea. Later steps will check the validity of what you do here. Later steps will refine it. But the essential work is done at this step. Limit your chosen topic. Swimming. Limit it to: Mark Spitz wouldn't make the finals if he were competing against today's stars. The backstroke is so effortless it is the best choice for staying afloat for long periods of time when survival demands it. The old swimming hole has disappeared from American adolescent culture. The Red Cross lifesaving program should concentrate more on prevention and less on the risky business of hauling persons out of the water. Now you've found the semblance of some controlling ideas on the topic of swimming.

Football: There has never been a better team than the Packers under Vince Lombardi. Football, while admittedly exciting, should be socially unacceptable because of its occasionally crippling violence. Professional football is about to follow the lead of college ball and adopt the wishbone as its basic offensive set. College players should be paid since they serve the school by their skills rather than learn skills from the school. That ninety-yard touchdown I scored in the tenth grade showed what a star I could have been if I had had better coaching and more opportunities.

By limiting the topic, we mean cutting it down from a general category to a specific statement regarding the general category. This is the difference between a topic and a controlling idea. A controlling idea is a specific statement to be developed. A topic is a broad area in which to look for ideas.

Right here, we are at the heart of the problem most people have in writing. They try to write from a topic instead of from the much more specific controlling idea. That is why writers become lost and never reach their destination. That is why their writing rambles instead of proceeding purposefully. And the change from topics to controlling ideas will make a writer out of you more quickly and more effectively than any other single thing you could do.

Obviously, there are other problems in writing. But the distinction between the topic and the controlling idea is one that we have found comes up again and again and ruins the efforts of many, many aspiring writers. If we were giving one piece of advice to a person who is trying to learn to write well, that advice would be exactly this: Write from controlling ideas, not from topics.

And, again, how do you convert a topic into a controlling idea? By the step we are talking about in this section. Limit the topic by making a specific statement, in sentence form, about it.

Once you have made that specific statement, set your controlling idea, you must ruthlessly decide what you will write by how it relates to that controlling idea. We will get into that later. But if you do, presto! you will find you can indeed write and probably write well. How well? The sky's the limit at this point. It is up to you. But at least you have taken that big step out of the realm of the fumbling and into the kingdom of the fluent.

Gather material

Once you have limited the chosen subject to the semblance of a controlling idea, your problems are not necessarily over. The next step is to begin gathering the material that you would like to include and that you think is relevant to the controlling idea. This step and the ones that follow not only supply you with the ideas you will use in the writing, they also serve as checks on the viability of your controlling idea. That idea, the statement of what you want to say about your chosen topic, may still not be in its final form. It is in workable form. Now you are checking it and refining it. Even if in the end you reject it, it will at least have served the purpose of leading you to the controlling idea you really want to use.

How do you gather material? From many possible sources, depending on the type of writing you are doing and depending on your controlling idea. The most common source is personal experience. What you see, know, have experienced, is the most fertile hunting grounds for supporting material. Reading and discussion with other people are also good areas. Libraries and the pronouncements of experts are the best and most accurate sources for specialized material already in the common and published body of knowledge.

List on a sheet of paper, or on file cards, what you know about your chosen controlling idea. List any written sources, books, magazine articles, journals, whatever you use. The nature of the topic will dictate how much you depend on others' ideas and how much you draw from personal experience. If you are writing a paper on why the Yankees lost the pennant, you probably will have to read nothing. But if you are tackling a thesis on the effect of brain waves on muscular activity, you will be buried in reference books. Most papers, though, will be a combination of formal research and of what you know, think, or have experienced on the topic.

The Red Cross lifesaving program should concentrate more on prevention and less on the risky business of hauling drowning persons out of the water. Why did you make that statement? Probably something happened to you that led to that conclusion. You saw, heard, or experienced something, or more likely a number of things, that made you think the controlling idea is true. List them. Then take a minute to stop at the library, look up lifesaving, and see what arguments the experts give for and against your position. List those also. Sometimes you need not look up everything in the field, but normally you should at least sample what those who know have to say on the subject. If you saw a television special on the subject, list the ideas presented in the program.

Select and evaluate

Now you have a list of the things you want to say about your controlling idea. Go carefully through the list, judging the value of each point by its importance to your controlling idea. There are two steps you will find you have to do as you proceed down the list.

First, you must discard all irrelevant and inappropriate material. No matter how brilliant and how true the statement, unless it contributes to the development of your controlling idea, it must be discarded. It requires discipline to throw out what does not belong. But it is the only way to write with maximum effectiveness.

Second, as you go down the list, keep an eye on the controlling idea itself. You may want to change or limit it further. For instance, you may find you have too much material on preventive lifesaving. You may want to limit the controlling idea further to something like: The Red Cross should demand that a person pass a course on how to avoid trouble in the water as well as one on lifesaving techniques before he receives his lifesaving certificate. It often happens that when you begin to think about or research a controlling idea that seemed limited, you find there is too much material. Limit it some more.

Reformulate the idea

This step flows naturally from the further limitation discussed above. Once you have looked over the material you have collected on your subject—both from your own knowledge and from expert sources—decide anew what the controlling idea should be. Forget the old idea. Pick the best controlling idea you can from analyzing the material. If the old and new ideas come out the same, fine. Often they will not.

Your material on the Red Cross lifesaving program likely will lead you to the conclusion that no matter how hard the Red Cross is working on preventive lifesaving, it still must teach techniques for pulling drowning persons from the water. You have ended up with a refined version that is contrary to your original controlling idea.

Finally, as the last step in the logical and classic way of selecting a controlling idea, organize the work you have done into a formal or informal outline. Weigh everything against the new controlling idea. Place your facts in order of importance, with less important supporting thoughts listed under the proper important supporting ideas. More of this in the next chapter, since this is the essence of converting material under a controlling idea into a written work.

One postscript about this invaluable method of reaching a good controlling idea. You may have to repeat the whole process more than once. As you refine the controlling idea, you may find that the material you have gathered no longer fits, or that the controlling idea is now so different there is more pertinent material both in your own experience and in outside sources. It is self-defeating, even suicidal, to refuse to recognize this. Extra work is involved, but there is no other way. You can't force either the material or the controlling idea. Admit again you are not ready to write yet, lay out the new version of the controlling idea, and start gathering the necessary material.

Write your way into a controlling idea

No matter what we say, no matter how much we emphasize the importance of solidifying the controlling idea before writing, most people will begin writing prematurely. You will start writing from a topic or from a weak controlling idea.

You will pay a price for doing so. This section is devoted to keeping that price reasonable, to making the best of your impatience. In this section we will try to harness your initial error of starting without an adequate controlling idea and to show you how to develop one as you go along. It is not the best way to do it. It is not even a good way. But it is a practical way, and a common one.

Because being forced to verbalize your thoughts will contribute to their clarification, this method can work. If you can't bear the thought of outlines and preassembled kits of material collected as above, you will try this method. We are trying here to divert the tendency of so many poor writers to plunge ahead into meaningless channels. We are hoping that at least before you are done you will find you have indeed worked out a controlling idea in the course of writing. Once you have written your way into that controlling idea, you have to go back and make sure all the preceding material supports it. It won't.

The reason so many people have to write their way into their controlling idea is that writers do not work in a vacuum. You will always seem to face limitations of time and distractions from within and without. So you often have to plunge in, eager to get started and hoping the writing will flow. It isn't until you get all tangled up that you realize you did not know what you wanted to say. That is the key moment. You can still sort yourself out. It is finally dawning on you what you were trying to say all along, what your controlling idea should have been.

Now you must apply the principles for selecting the controlling idea. You must stop and write out in a simple sentence what it is you are trying to accomplish by this writing.

If you stop at this point (and it may be two sentences or twenty pages into the writing) and lay that controlling idea out on paper in front of you, you can still save the writing. If you don't, don't say you do not know how to write when it doesn't work out.

Now comes the characteristic step of this third process for finding the controlling idea. Rewrite. Once the controlling idea has developed out of the writing, start over. Be willing to throw away everything that went before.

Stop. Think. Analyze. Shut out the past. Shut out what you have written. Proceed logically to express the newly clarified controlling idea in a piece of writing.

Develop a new rough draft, using the controlling idea to guide, dictate, restrict, unify, as any good controlling idea always does. Apply all the principles you will learn in Chapter Three for developing a controlling idea into a piece of writing.

Use your original rough draft only as a source, along with many other sources of material. Check it for lesser supporting ideas that can be carried over to the development of the new controlling idea.

So again, by a completely different method—or is it?— you have reached a solid controlling idea. That is the important thing. But the same warning must be sounded again. You must be willing to apply the process all over if necessary. As you write from this new controlling idea, you may still find the work wandering and getting lost. You may find yourself tending towards a new idea. If the controlling idea continues to change, change with it.

Summary

In the end, it does not matter how you reach a good controlling idea. The important thing is to have it and to use it to guide your work to an effective conclusion. Which of the three methods for selecting the controlling idea you learn to use most successfully depends on your personality and your stage of advancement in the writing process. All three are results oriented. So whichever gets the best results for you is the one for you to use.

The important thing is the clear controlling idea, not the process by which you reached it.

CHAPTER THREE

Developing the Controlling Idea

You have formulated a good, workable controlling idea. You sit down to convert it into a piece of writing and . . . And what? Many would-be writers come up against a wide chasm at this point. How do you get from a controlling idea on the north rim of the Grand Canyon to an acceptable finished work way over there on the south horizon?

There is a bridge up there, you know. And once you find the bridge, you will also find the valley is not as big as it looked.

In this chapter, we are going to study the construction of that simple little bridge across the chasm. The bridge has a name on it: organization.

Organization

Don't try to jump immediately from the controlling idea to the finished writing. Instead, do a little planning ahead. Think over what you want to say. What points do you want to make?

As we said in the previous chapter, the material you want to use to support your controlling idea comes basically from two sources: what you already know, and what you can learn from outside. Begin your organizing by laying out the material you have available from these two sources and arranging it in an effective order.

This chapter contains two major ideas, both geared to crossing that chasm between the controlling idea and the writing. They are the pillars that hold up the bridge. The first section contains information on how to arrange material logically. The second is on how to achieve emphasis and effectiveness through the orderly presentation of the material.

Outlines

To insure that your material is well organized in support of your controlling idea, you need an outline. An outline is the best tool for establishing and maintaining an effective organization of your material.

Unfortunately, outlines have a bad image. Most writers and would-be writers have learned to hate outlines somewhere along the way. Many will go to great lengths to avoid having to compose outlines.

That is regrettable. Outlines are really such helpful, accommodating creatures. They are handmaids and workhorses, not prima donnas or thoroughbreds.

They are hated for two reasons. First, they require discipline. A successful outline contains all pertinent information properly arranged. It is easier to just start in and hope the material will fall into place. Secondly, writers often tackle the outline before they have collected the material. They wander through, trying to think up enough Roman numerals and ones and twos and a)s and b)s. That is backwards. They should compile and list their thoughts and information first. Then the outline flows easily.

An outline, then, is simply the arrangement of your thoughts on a controlling idea into a logical order of large and small supporting points.

Here are the simple steps to an effective outline.

Supporting ideas

We have already talked about this. The things you want to say are either in your head or in the notes you have taken. Write them down in any order.

Important supporting ideas

Rate your ideas as important or less important. Important supporting ideas should substantially advance your controlling idea. When you know which ideas are the important ones for you, arrange them in order of importance, chronological order, or some other logical series. (See the next section of this chapter for effective arrangements.)

Less important supporting ideas

The less important ideas—the ones you have left over after you have taken out the important ones—are used to flesh out the important supporting ideas. They should become supporting ideas for the important ideas. Many of them are probably illustrations and examples. Look them over and first of all, reject completely those that do not seem to have a place under the important supporting ideas. They probably are not to the point of your controlling idea. Then place the remaining ones under the appropriate important supporting idea. You will want to develop at greater length the important ideas you have written down. At this point you are outlining, not developing the ideas. But the small ideas you list will furnish you with useful examples and supporting arguments.

The more complete the outline, the more small ideas you will place under the big ones.

Arrange in logical order

After you have judged all the thoughts and placed all the small ones under each big point, make sure that all the points are in the order in which you want to use them. Recommended orders will be given in the next section of this chapter.

Summary on outlines

So there you have it. Just that easily, the outline is completed. If you have not experienced the pleasure and confidence that comes from writing from a good outline, you are about to.

Outline example

Already in Chapter One, while illustrating a different point, we have gone through the process of laying out facts and arranging them into an outline. We will do it again here with a different controlling idea so that you can see how easy and effective an outline is. We have intentionally chosen a controlling idea with many supporting thoughts so you can see how something that originally looks like chaos can be brought to functioning order by simple logical steps.

Let us use as an example one of the controlling ideas we developed in Chapter Two: No matter how hard the Red Cross is working on preventive lifesaving, it still must teach techniques for pulling drowning persons from the water.

What supporting statements do we have that we want to include under that controlling idea? Our first step in organization is to list them in any order. Here are some that might come to mind:

1. Thousands of persons drown in the U.S.A. every year, but thousands more experience narrow escapes because of the vigilance of persons trained in lifesaving techniques.

2. Water-skiers can be knocked out when they fall.

3. Water is essentially a foreign and dangerous medium for man to enter.

4. Small children cannot be expected to have the judgment of adults.

5. The Red Cross has come a long way in educating the public on the dangers of boating and swimming.

6. At some point, laws are needed to force precautions on the general public.

7. A certain number of people will be faced with the choice of ignoring safety precautions or staying away from the water—and will choose to take the risk of ignoring precautions.

8. Many children die each summer because they were not wearing life preservers around boats.

9. Even an expert lifesaver can have trouble trying to save a panicked and struggling swimmer.

10. Many of those around lakes in summer are persons who do not live near water and thus are not included in the normal audience reached by preventive-education efforts. They are vacationers who spend two weeks a year near the water.

11. It is almost impossible to police our lakes and beaches adequately.

12. Even a capsized boat should float; and it is safer to remain with the boat than to try to swim to shore.

13. Mouth-to-mouth resuscitation has many emergency uses besides helping to revive a victim of drowning.

14. Most lakes are in parks, rural, wilderness or remote areas, far from trained medics and emergency rescue equipment.

15. Even if preventive education reached everyone, in

this imperfect world people would still forget, ignore, or decide to break the rules.

16. Allowance would always have to be made for accidents and problems that develop despite all precautions.

Sixteen statements on lifesaving. Confusing? The next
step is to analyze them and arrange them in a logical sequence
of large and small supporting ideas. The key here, as in all
aspects of writing, is to NOT LOSE SIGHT OF THE CON-
TROLLING IDEA. In this case we should keep in mind that
we are not trying to prove the Red Cross does indeed engage
in preventive education. Neither are we trying to show what
the Red Cross teaches in its lifesaving courses. Our controlling
idea is that preventive education will never be enough. Our
supporting ideas, then, will demonstrate this.

With that in mind, from our list the following statements
qualify as reasons why lifesaving must be taught, that is, as
important supporting ideas:

1. Thousands of persons drown in the U.S.A. every year,
but thousands more experience narrow escapes because of
the vigilance of persons trained in lifesaving techniques.

4. Small children cannot be expected to have the judgment of adults.

7. A certain number of people will be faced with the
choice of ignoring safety precautions or staying away from
the water—and will choose to take the risk of ignoring precautions.

10. Many of those around lakes in summer are persons
who do not live near water and thus are not included in the
normal audience reached by preventive-education efforts.

15. Even if preventive education reached everyone, in
this imperfect world, people would still forget, ignore or decide to break the rules.

16. Allowance would always have to be made for accidents and problems that develop despite all precautions.

What of the rest of the statements? If they are not important supporting ideas, they must be either less important ideas or they are not pertinent and should not be included in the writing. Take them one by one and decide what to do with them.

Statement 2 is clearly an example (lesser supporting idea) for statement 16. Make it a supporting idea for 16.

Statement 3 also supports statement 16.

Statement 5, while true, is assumed in the controlling idea. There is no reason for including it as a separate point. It can be dropped.

Statement 6, upon examination, will be found not to be pertinent to this controlling idea. It could be a separate controlling idea for a different piece of writing, but it would only lead away from this controlling idea. Drop it.

Statement 8 is an example of statement 4.

Statement 9 is clearly not pertinent to this controlling idea. Neither is statement 11, which seems to be related to rejected statement 6.

Statement 12 is an example of what can be learned in preventive education classes, but we are not dealing with that here, so drop it.

Statement 13 is also not pertinent to our controlling idea. It brings up a new idea.

Finally, statement 14 also surprisingly does not apply to our controlling idea. It deals with why both prevention and lifesaving are necessary and that is a slightly different controlling idea. This statement is the closest to being pertinent of those we are rejecting. It is one that could go either way, but a good rule of thumb is unless it clearly has to stay you are better off getting rid of it.

So now we have made some progress. We have isolated six important supporting ideas and have thrown out six statements as not pertinent to our controlling idea. Now the material looks much more manageable.

The only step left is to arrange the important supporting ideas into an outline. In this case, let's decide which of the supporting ideas is most important and work back to the least important. Putting the lesser supporting ideas under the appropriate important ones, we will end up with the following functional outline:

I. (Controlling idea) No matter how hard the Red Cross is working on preventive lifesaving, it still must teach techniques for pulling drowning persons from the water.

  1. Allowance would always have to be made for accidents and problems that develop despite all precautions.

    a. Water is essentially a foreign and dangerous medium for men to enter.

    b. Water-skiers can be knocked out when they fall.

  2. Even if preventive education reached everyone, some people would ignore, forget, or decide to break the rules.

  3. Many of those around lakes in summer are persons who do not live near water and thus are not included in the normal audience reached by preventive-education efforts. (For instance, vacationers from the cities.)

  4. A certain number of people will be faced with the choice of ignoring safety precautions or staying away from the water—and will choose to risk ignoring precautions.

  5. Small children are a special case, since they are attracted to water but cannot be expected to understand the implications of preventive education. For instance, many children die each summer because they were not wearing life preservers in boats.

  6. Evidence is against preventive education being enough. The fact is, thousands of persons drown in the U.S.A.

every year and thousands more experience narrow escapes because of the vigilance of other persons trained
in lifesaving techniques.

Organizing for emphasis

Listing and explaining the principal ideas under a controlling
idea makes what you are trying to say clear. To make your
point emphatically, however, concentrate on the order in
which you state your arguments or ideas.

The rule for obtaining emphasis through the order in
which you list your points is ridiculously simple: There are
two emphatic positions, the beginning and the end. That's
it. That's the whole key to achieving emphasis through organization. Take your best argument, your best idea, your strongest point, and put it at the beginning or at the end.

When should you put it at the beginning and when at
the end? That depends on the circumstances—what you are
trying to accomplish, for whom you are writing, etc.

The rule is: If you are going to have trouble keeping
your readers' attention, hit them hard immediately. Don't
let them get away. If, on the other hand, you have their attention but want to convince them, keep your best material for
last.

Let's work in terms of an example.

You are recommending to your boss that he buy a small
computer to handle billing records. Your controlling idea is:
Buying a small billing computer would make this a better
business.

Your reasons are:

1. Errors cause unhappy customers and loss of future
business.
2. The salaries of three clerks could be eliminated at an

annual savings of $30,000, the total cost of the computer.

3. As the business expands, no additions to staff will be necessary because the computer has almost limitless capacity.

4. The same computer, with a different program disc, could be used to keep inventory and control stock.

5. It looks good to bill by computer. The public takes it as a sign of a professionally run business.

Your best argument is that it will increase profits by $30,000 a year after the first year. Where do you put it?

Strongest idea first

Your boss is a busy man with one hundred things on his mind. The important thing is to get and hold his attention and interest. And nothing holds his interest better than a chance to increase profits. So lead with your strongest punch.

"We can save $30,000 a year by buying a small computer to handle billing for us.

"That is only one of several advantages to having an in-house computer. Some others are:

"If we buy a second programming disc (they are cheap) we could also solve the always-troublesome problem of inventory and supply by having the computer keep track of them.

"Errors on bills could be eliminated—and you know how angry customers become when they receive an incorrect bill.

"As we expand, the computer will become more important and save more money because it will have the capacity to expand with us without necessitating additional overhead.

"Marketing experts say computer billing is taken by the public as a sign of professionalism. It would enhance our image and encourage public trust."

Get his attention and keep it. Go from strongest to weakest.

The same applies to sales efforts, complaints, contract discussions, almost any relationship between professionals who are interested only in substance. Come right to the point. Give them a reason for listening to you.

From strongest to weakest is also often the best way to proceed in dealing with literary topics, or when writing for students or the general public. Any work aimed at browsers or casual readers should hit hard immediately. If it does not, they will move on. The reader may not look at the second paragraph if the first one is not strong enough.

Journalism operates constantly on this theory. The "lead" or first sentence in journalism carries the strongest material in the story. The details can come later; the essentials must be up front. Otherwise, the reader will turn to another article without ever learning the substance of the story.

"An armed gunman held a small army of policemen at bay for three hours this morning, wounding two officers and terrifying scores of residents before surrendering peacefully." The reader will want to read on for details.

"At 10:05 this morning, the police received a call requesting assistance in settling a family dispute on Maple Street." The story is the same, but with that lead the reader will never get to the part about the seven shotguns and the bullets whizzing overhead.

Debating and most argumentative writing often bring out the heavy artillery immediately. This form of writing, though, has a serious weakness. The weakness lies in the fact that each supporting idea is weaker than the one before. The reader gradually tends to lose interest. In the example of the small computer, the writer counts on his opener to generate enough interest to hold his boss all the way through. No detail will be insignificant to a boss who is seriously considering a money-saving suggestion. In the case of the newspaper article, the reader will move on when he has as much information as he wants.

But such writing will not always work. Sometimes—many

times—using your best material first is not the best way to present a controlling idea.

And that brings us to the second emphatic position.

Strongest idea last

Let's change our scenario a little. You are not trying to sell your boss on a computer. He has come to you and asked you to make a recommendation on the practicality of a computer for his operation. You don't have to catch and hold his interest. What you have to do now is convince him that a small computer is what he wants. You want to present to him the strongest case possible.

When holding interest is not paramount, there is a better way to present arguments or ideas than to hit with the strongest. Reverse the order. *End* with the strongest. Start with the weakest. This is known as the climactic order, because it starts slowly and builds to a final climax. If the boss is going to read the memo anyway and you want to leave him convinced, let him end with the best and have the strongest reasons on his mind when he is finished.

Using the same controlling idea and the same five arguments, you would construct your memo along these lines:

"Marketing experts say computer billing is taken by the public as a sign of professionalism. A small computer would enhance our image with customers and encourage public trust.

"As our business grows, with a computer we would not have to add to the staff. Even small computers have more capacity than we would need for decades.

"We could eliminate errors in our billing system—and you know how many problems have been caused by billing errors and angry customers.

"Also, that same computer, with another inexpensive

disc, could also be used to straighten out our nagging inventory and supply problems.

"But best of all, the computer will save us money— $30,000 annually after the first year."

Note that the key difference which allows you to use the powerful climactic approach is that your audience is interested enough to hear you out. When you have to hold his attention, use the best arguments first. When you have his attention but want to prove your point, use the best arguments last.

Salesmen face both situations and must be able to adjust from one approach to the other. The basic rule is the same. When the customer is interested, you can afford the luxury of the climactic approach. When you are trying to get him interested, lead off with the heavy artillery.

Thus, the sales material you leave in a customer's office for him to browse through must hit hard immediately. After he is interested he can investigate the small points. But the filmstrip presentation that you give for customers who have requested information on their own should take the climactic approach.

We have established the principles through one example, but they apply to all decisions on order of presentation. Another simple but helpful rule is: Any time you have a captive audience, start light and end heavy. Thus if you are preparing a speech for a luncheon or a seminar, if you are writing a training manual for office personnel, or if you are giving a written warning to a recalcitrant employee, use the climactic approach.

We are talking here only about nonfiction writing. Fiction plays by its own rules, including a basis in chronological order, but in general the climactic approach is the best in fiction. Many beginners think the chronological approach is the heart of fiction. Not so. Since the material is not factual, you can use any order you want. And you can and should vary the chronology to meet the needs of drama. Can you imagine a murder mystery that does not hold back the most important developments?

Strong ideas at both ends

Many times, maybe most times, you will be writing in circumstances in which you feel the double need to create interest and to finish strongly. Maybe you do not know whether your reader is interested enough to allow you to use the climactic order. Your client has shown a spark of interest but you have to lure him in further. For any number of reasons you could be uneasy with the climactic approach but still not want to use up all of your ammunition too soon.

There is an easy solution. Save the best argument until last, but use the second-best first. Or vice versa. Then scatter the rest of the arguments alternately through the body of the work. This approach tends both to hold interest and maintain effectiveness. It is a compromise solution, however, and should be used only when you feel you must accomplish both goals of holding interest and leaving a strong impression.

Consider our example again. Order it this way:

"A billing computer could save us money—at least $30,000 a year.

"It could also eliminate the errors that have been plaguing our bills and costing us customer goodwill.

"Along the same line, studies show that computer billing enhances the company's image with the public because the public reads it as professional.

"Of course, in a small company such as ours, a computer would have ample capacity to allow us to expand without additional billing expenses.

"But, perhaps most interesting for our purposes, that

same computer could be used by the supply department to control inventory and maintain even flow of materials—another money-saving option."

Weighing appeal and importance

There is an effective variation on the technique of balancing important supporting ideas at both ends of the writing. That is to rate the ideas not only by importance but also by reader interest. Then put the most telling arguments last, but put the most appealing first.

This method is commonly used by essayists, newspaper and magazine feature writers, speechmakers and most professional communicators. It is almost a routine, standard trick of effective writing. It is simple and easy to use and it works wonders. How many suspense novels include a sex scene in the second chapter? How many magazine features start with an example? How many sermons start with a story and end with a moral?

Summary

The rules for arranging the supporting ideas under a controlling idea are simple and easy to follow. The beginnings and the ends are the most important parts of a work. Circumstances dictate whether you use powerful beginnings, powerful endings, or both.

In any case, be very aware of beginnings and endings. That is where the effort and polish must be applied if you are going to write effectively. That is where the controlling idea is put across to the reader.

And if you are working from a strong controlling idea and putting it across effectively, you are a good writer.

It is no less simple—and no simpler—than that.

CHAPTER FOUR

Be Specific

So far in this book, we have been dealing with how you prepare to write, how you settle on what you want to say, and how you develop your thoughts effectively. Specifically, we have been trying to emphasize the importance of a clear controlling idea to guide the writing. We have talked about what a controlling idea is, what it does, how it aids in effective writing, what the dangers and problems of not using a controlling idea are, how you can formulate a controlling idea of your own, and how the controlling idea dictates the organization of the writing.

Now we are going to begin talking about the actual writing. Many of the problems of writing are negative ones. Those trying to write are simply doing something wrong that is keeping their writing from being effective. We feel that to be a good, effective writer, you do not need to know everything about writing. You do have to know how to avoid the basic and common errors that weaken writing.

The first of these is the error of being too general.

Specific is more meaningful

One easy way to make immense improvement in your writing is to be as specific as possible at all times. Too many writers try to dress up their language and their thoughts when they put them down on paper. They resort to a formal style that deals in generalities rather than in direct terms and is therefore clumsy and unclear. Their writing bears no resemblance to their spoken word or their thought patterns.

Check yourself. You probably have trouble expressing yourself in writing because you are not writing what you are thinking. You are "dressing it up." In doing so, you may be losing one of the most important qualities of good writing—specificity.

Being specific is an asset that constantly stands writers in good stead. It is one of those little tricks that make a tremendous difference in writing.

What do we mean by being specific? Specific means that which is individual, particular, or distinguishing about anything. The word comes from "species," a term indicating the most complete division, most individual description possible short of unique. A mammal is more specific than an animal. A great ape is more specific than a mammal. A man is more specific than a great ape. And Robert C. Dudley III is more specific than a man.

In writing, use the most specific term possible short of inaccuracy in all circumstances.

The opposite of specific is general. Using general words in writing weakens the writing by cutting down on clarity. A general term covers many more possibilities and the reader must try to sort out what specifically you mean. So meaning is best conveyed through specific writing, through the choice of words that are limited in meaning to what you want to convey to the reader.

The specific is much easier to write, as well as being clearer. But most beginning and unpracticed writers, perhaps because of pretensions at expertise, feel they have to leave the specific world of everyday speech and enter the general world when they pick up a pen. It is an error for which they pay dearly.

In speech you say, "Sally has a bug. Her nose has been running all day, she has the chills, her face is flushed, and she won't eat." Why then, in writing, do you simply say, "Sally has been ill?"

In writing you say, "The car broke down." In speech you say, "I heard this whistling, steam began pouring out of the front of the car, the red light went on on the dashboard, and the engine conked out."

Don't write, "She is a hypochondriac" when you can say, "She took aspirin for headaches she never got but feared she might get. Then she read that aspirins were making her stomach bleed, although she had seen no evidence of this. So she began taking bufferin for the headaches she never got and milk to coat the stomach she had not noticed was bleeding."

Which of the following paragraphs attracts you more? Which is more clear, more effective?

"With the constantly increasing price of gasoline, a new trend in entertainment is developing in this country. More and more people are spending more and more time at shopping malls but buying less and less. They are going to entertain themselves rather than to purchase items."

Or:

"Eight-year-old Sally Thomson and her little brother Timmy love to go to the beach. But they do not go as often as they used to, even in midsummer. The beach is forty miles away. Now on hot evenings they drive four miles to the shopping mall. There they wander through the stores, looking for bargains, stopping for pizza or an ice cream cone, playing with the puppies and kittens in the pet shop, and fingering the stuffed pandas and Barbie dolls in the toy department. Sally and Timmy are victims of the rising price of fuel. So are the merchants in the mall, because millions of Americans are doing exactly what the Thomson family is doing. They are taking their entertainment together in the air-conditioned mall, instead of at the beach, the mountains, the campsites, the parks, the cities, the museums, or the ballparks. They are saving gas. But they are not visiting the mall to buy; they are visiting it for entertainment. And the merchants are not furnishing entertainment; they are trying to sell. So the parking lots are crowded, but the stores are going broke."

The two paragraphs say almost the same thing, but the second one is specific.

One more example, because all the above examples are longer in the specific version. That is not always the case. It was so in our examples because we were emphasizing the use of the specific. Consider the following:

"Pecuniary insufficiency tempers at times even the most well-intentioned. Even though momentary, there are times when no amount of goodwill can affect what circumstances have decreed shall occur. Those who ride the waves occasionally find themselves in the troughs and can only wait for the currents to lift them again."

How about, "I'm broke. I'll pay you next payday."

Specific is more interesting

Pick up your local newspaper any day and read the first few paragraphs of any news or feature article. Notice the plethora of facts. Facts are by nature specific. Notice how the feature stories lead with a quote or an incident that capsulizes what the feature is about. Notice how the stories deal entirely in specifics.

Specifics are the stock in trade of newspapers. Much newspaper writing is not that good, but it is specific. It is heavy on facts and details, and that makes it interesting. Newspapers consistently offer good examples of specific writing.

Now pick up a government report, a politician's speech, a scientific treatise. Notice the difference. Notice the lack of specifics, the vague and boring generalities. And make up your mind always to write with the lively sense of detail shown by reporters rather than the boringly complicated generalities of studies and government reports.

"It appears to be a function of the mind to simplify the complex problems so as to more easily deal with them. Frequently these simplifications merely focus in on the more visible aspects of the problem and, as a result, a fraction of the reasons for a dilemma end up receiving all the blame."

Compare that to some routine newspaper leads:

"The school board has been stopped from hiring anyone to replace Main Street School administrator John Hopkins. Superior Court Judge Brian Mullens issued the order Friday."

" 'I'm scared. I'm so scared,' cried seventy-eight-old Mrs. Edna Bowen Friday, as police tried to evacuate her from a building on the roof of which a lone man with a rifle watched the street below. 'I have a bad heart, and I can't run. Couldn't I just hide here in the basement?' "

We have stereotyped news stories and bureaucratese to make a point. The point is, everyone reads the specific. Nobody struggles through the general. You want your writing to be read and enjoyed, to be effective. Use the specific. It is livelier and much more interesting.

Specific helps the reader visualize

It is time for a little digression into common sense and the process of understanding.

We learn new things by relating them to ideas already in our minds, or by joining two known facts in unlikely or novel combinations. The need for being specific in writing is based upon how the mind works. There is only one way to learn something new, and that is to relate it to something known. Make sure, when talking about something unknown, that you talk in terms and context the reader understands.

A computer instructor, talking about the storage capacity of a three million megabyte disc to a group of secretaries, will say something like this:

"Think in terms of a large room filled with filing cabinets. There are 250 filing drawers in those cabinets. Each drawer holds sixty separate file folders. And each folder holds 100 sheets of paper.

"One hundred secretaries will be using the computer. Each one will have two filing drawers. That will mean each secretary has 120 folders, each folder capable of holding 100 invoices, 100 bills, or 100 stock lists. That's 12,000 different pieces of paper each secretary can file away and retrieve instantly.

"There are also fifty extra file drawers available for anyone who needs more room.

"You don't want the other secretaries looking into your files, or changing the entries, so we will put a lock on each file drawer. The key to that lock is called the access code. It is like the combination of a safe. Only someone who knows the access code can get into each file. The key to open the lock on each file drawer will be the last four digits of the social security number of the person designated to use the drawer."

To secretaries, computer megabytes are incomprehensible. But they are thoroughly familiar with file folders, a very specific object. By talking in terms of a specific thing with which the secretaries are totally familiar, the computer expert led them to a functional understanding of how to use the computer.

All communication is based on this process of leading the learner (reader) from a known specific to an unknown. Writing is one of the most basic ways of communication. To communicate successfully and effectively through writing, use the specific.

Areas to be specific

In a word, you must be specific everywhere.

There are three areas where many writers run into problems.

Words and sentences

Being specific starts with individual words and sentences. It comes down to saying exactly what you mean. There is always the temptation to sound a little more sophisticated, a little more polished. So you avoid the word that comes to mind naturally. And the new word makes your thought a little less clear, because the meaning is not as precise. Very often the word you choose because of its polish is a more general one. Don't. Choose the exact word; make it as specific as possible without losing the meaning.

If you are driving a car, don't call it a vehicle. If it is a station wagon, why call it a car? If you need typing paper and erasers, you don't put in a requisition for office supplies. You don't need paper clips, rubber bands, envelopes, and invoices. You put in a requisition for typing paper and erasers. Be specific and get what you want. If there are thirty-seven employees in your firm, why say you employ "some thirty" employees? "After we ate, we played games." No. "After the hot dogs, beans, and lemonade, we started a softball game in the field above the river."

Start being specific at the lowest level. Start with the word and the sentence, and watch your writing come to life.

Examples and illustrations

Being specific in examples would seem to go without saying. What else is an example but a specific statement about a generality? The problem is the choice of bad examples. Many examples are nothing more than new generalities or restatements of the generality. Many more do not prove the point, which is the same as picking the wrong word.

Industrial chemicals are polluting our drinking water. That is a general statement. An estimated 20,000 rivers are too polluted to drink from. That seems like an example, but it is not. It is a restatement of the same generality. Pine Lake in central Wisconsin, with a fertilizer processing plant on its shore, was found to contain so much poison even the trees ten miles away were dying. That is an example.

Free enterprise is the best way to control inflation (a general statement). For example, the garment industry is one of the most competitive in the country and clothing prices rose only 2.5 percent last year. On the other hand, petroleum is a highly regulated industry and oil prices went up 110 percent during the same period (specific examples).

Abstract material

The third area where writers tend to have problems with specificity is when they are dealing with abstract material. When the subject itself is most abstract, it is toughest for the writer to be specific. That, however, is when it is most important.

"Economic indicators show that the country may be headed for a recession. This would be a good time for our company to begin stockpiling supplies that could run short later. We should also avoid building new facilities and limit our hiring of new staff. There are other ways of saving money during a recession and we should do them all."

The above is not an atypical memo. Such generalities often pass for astute thinking, but they are ineffective as means of communication. The writer did not know the value of being specific when dealing with abstract material. Here is a specific memo on the same subject:

"The prime interest rate has risen another half of one percent, the third rise this quarter. Income from total goods and services fell 3.3 percent this quarter, which would equate to an annual rate of 13.2 percent. Gross national product is rising less than normal by about 4 percent. So it looks as if a recession is on the way. We deal in plumbing fixtures. During previous recessions, the steel business has been one of the hardest hit. Another industry that quickly develops problems during a recession is the appliance industry.

"I recommend we cut back on our stock of pipe, fittings, casings and fixtures which are made from iron and steel. No sense carrying a big inventory if the suppliers are crying out for business and can fill our orders quickly.

"Furthermore, those retail outlets in the Northeast and

that assembly plant in Columbus should be reconsidered. Will we need them? Are they good investments in view of the fact that a recession historically brings a drop in our business?

"If things really get bad, we can anticipate layoffs, so we should begin cutting staff through attrition, at least until we see the trend more clearly."

The second memo deals in specifics even though it is trying to establish some abstract and general principles. It is far clearer and much more effective.

Accuracy in specifics

A couple of warnings about specifics are in order. They arise from the fact that specifics zero in so accurately on what you are trying to say. There is less margin for error when you are writing in specifics and that can be a problem.

One of the reasons so much general writing takes place is because it is more vague. And the more vague the writing, the less careful the writer has to be. If you say "Economic indicators are down," you do not have to look anything up. You can write it instantly. If you say "Goods and services are off 3.3 percent; the gross national product has slowed by 4 percent; the interest rate has risen one and a half percent in the past quarter," you must be sure. You will probably have to dig out copies of the *Wall Street Journal,* government reports, and *Business Review.* That will take time. So many people simply write "Economic indicators are down" and let it go. And in doing so they sap the strength and effectiveness out of their writing.

Equally dangerous is the tendency to take a chance in writing. You think you remember that figure was 3.6 percent. So that is the specific you use. But actually it was 6.3 percent. Now you have a problem, an even more serious one than the laziness that had you writing general statements. To guarantee that your writing reaches the right conclusion, that is, presents the controlling idea in the most effective way, the writing must not only be specific, it must also be accurate. The specifics must be true. There is no substitute for this accuracy, even if it means a little extra digging in the library.

Proving your point

When your facts and examples are accurate, however, you still have only done part of your work. There is another danger to look out for. Those specifics must prove what you want them to, explain what you want explained. They must bring the reader to acceptance and understanding of the controlling idea. The mere fact that they are accurate does not mean they prove the point. Make sure your specifics draw the reader towards, not away from, the controlling idea. Make sure your specifics, especially if they are examples, fit.

What we are saying here is something we already stressed in dealing with the controlling idea. The controlling idea dictates all the material included in the writing. Only what supports the controlling idea can be included. And a specific idea that is not to the point does not advance the controlling idea.

It may be true in the plumbing business that a recession hurts production. But in the newspaper business, the opposite is true. The worse off people are, the more they want to know what is happening, the more they search the want ads, the more they read the grocery ads to find the lowest prices, the more merchants advertise to draw customers. You cannot use the coming recession to support a controlling idea that your newspaper should cut back on production. Your specifics do not prove your controlling idea, no matter how accurate they are.

Skiing is an expensive sport. Boots can cost $100. Skis

cost at least as much; poles are another $30; jackets run around $70; lift fees are $15, and discount rates are available for students. The last fact does not support your controlling idea.

Summary

Always use the specific, even if it means more research. It will add vitality and interest to your writing. But make sure your specifics are accurate and promote the controlling idea. Specifics will pay heavy dividends in the quality of your writing and in the value other people will place on it.

CHAPTER FIVE

Be Simple
and Direct

There is a gap between the way people talk and the way people write.

There should be such a gap. Writing is a more permanent, more thoughtful, more studied method of communicating than speech. It requires a different style. We firmly believe in the importance of literary language and the protection of written communication as a separate art form from the spoken word.

Does that complicate the task of writing? No. The human mind is fully capable of adjusting. The written word is what the spoken word would be if the speaker had the time to think out what he wanted to say, work it over, polish it, until it was in the best possible form. There is no intrinsic difference. The difference is in polish. You speak as you go along, with little chance to correct before presentation. These corrections, which should greatly improve the clarity and effectiveness of the thought, make the written word different from the spoken.

The problem people have with writing simply and directly is deeper than that. When many people try to write, what comes out is not a polished version of the way they would speak. With many problems of writers, it is not that they don't write as they talk; it is that they don't write as they think. They turn artificial. They present their thoughts in a way that bears little resemblance to either their speaking pattern or their thinking pattern. They try to be formal. They try to be erudite. They try to be clever. They lose the greatest asset of both spoken and written communication: naturalness.

Why does the thought process so often remain natural when transferred to the spoken word, but become artificial when transferred to the written word?

One reason—the one that concerns us here—is that writers expect too much of their written word. They want to show themselves as something they are not. They consciously or unconsciously try to portray themselves in writing as more than they actually are. To do that, they try to enhance their writing into something beyond themselves. They do not do so when they talk, because they do not have the opportunity. But when they write, they have more time to work their writing into whatever form they want it to be or whatever they want to portray themselves as. The result is artificiality. Another result is lack of clarity and effectiveness.

They are forgetting an important aspect of writing. Writing is a way of communicating thoughts first of all. Only secondarily and incidentally does it communicate personality. (Furthermore, if the purpose of a piece of writing is to convey personality instead of thought, what is the point of conveying a personality that is not yours? The result—except in the specialized case of a fiction writer writing through the eyes of an imaginary first person—is usually a totally predictable muddle.)

The problem is complicated further because so much writing that we see around us has still another purpose, namely to confuse, distort, or mislead. There are many clever writers who have a real interest in not being clear and direct. Promoters, politicians, salesmen, public relations directors, ad men, bureaucrats are just a few of the many members of society who have much to gain by exaggerating or distorting the truth. If you are trying to sell a product that is basically the same as seven other brands of the same product, you will have to find a gimmick, distort the picture in some way, exaggerate, to do it.

Much of the writing we run into today, from advertising copy to politicians' speeches, is a bad model for aspiring writers. It is intentionally or unintentionally poor writing. It is above all not to be emulated. Intentional obscurity and vagueness are so prevalent that they seem to be standards for writing when in actuality they are to be scorned rather than copied.

Simple, direct writing enlightens and clarifies. It is easy to read, intelligible, interesting. And it is easier to write than the pompous and fancy styles so many writers try to use to express themselves.

How do you attain simple and direct writing? Say what you are thinking in the words you are thinking. There is no special secret because it is the natural way of expressing yourself. It is the other kind of writing that takes work and tricks. And that is not worth learning.

Writing is the expression of exactly what you are thinking. There are, however, numerous areas where despite your best efforts you are liable to fall into the trap of unnecessary pomposity or obscurity. In this chapter, we will talk about a number of the more common ways in which writers destroy their simplicity and directness and therefore their clarity and effectiveness. We will go over some ways of insuring that your style is simple and direct.

"I conversed with you Friday on the telephone about a matter of great importance and promise to both of us. I am speaking of the very high profits to be made from a highly perceptive and extraordinary business transaction from which we could both benefit in the not-so-distant future. As I indicated in our previous conversation over the phone, I have come into possession of a highly desirable and strategically located real estate parcel that could readily be dissected into magnificent sections with water frontage and aquatic leisure opportunities if you could invest with me a small sum necessary to do a limited amount of improvements. Earth-moving equipment would have to be used to rearrange the contours through artificial formation of plateaus and troughs. Such improvements would afford us the opportunity of resale at a price many times the present worth of the land."

Did you understand that passage? Say it simply and directly:

"As I said Friday, I've got some swamp land. What I don't have is the $25,000 necessary to bulldoze the lowest area, pile the sand up onto the higher sections, and thus create a lake and elevated lots which could be sold for waterfront homes. Will you put up the money for a share of the profits?"

It is amazing the amount of extra work writers cause themselves by saying too much. It is so much easier and simpler just to state what you want to say. Yet the temptation to overwrite is almost irresistible and is the cause of much of the poor writing that frustrates would-be authors.

Unnecessary words

The starting point for simple, direct writing is the building block for all writing, the word. Go back over your work each time and take out all unnecessary words. You will be surprised how many you have put in that you do not need. It is an eye-opening exercise.

You will also find that once you realize you are going to have to go back and remove them later, you will be much more careful about what you put in in the first place. The exercise of going back not only improves what you have written, it improves what you will write in the future by making you aware that you are not writing as simply and directly as you could, you are tending towards wordiness. The more you go back over what you write, the less necessary it will be to do so. You will find yourself writing more simply, directly, and effectively.

The easiest way to achieve simple and direct writing is the mechanical exercise of forcing yourself to go back through what you have written and ruthlessly cross out every unnecessary word. That exercise will soon have you keeping unnecessary words out of your original copy.

What words do you look for? What words are likely to be excess baggage?

Adjectives

Adjectives are often the biggest offenders in wordiness. Adjectives perform a function. They aid in description. The red chair. The tall woman. The towering and majestic mountains. But they also often are not necessary. The rule is: Use adjectives only when the omission of them could make the writing obscure or incomplete, only when the description cannot stand without them.

"He was small and wiry, quick on his feet and quick of wit. When he walked, his narrow hips swayed and his bony shoulders hunched forward eagerly." The sentence is filled with adjectives, but they are necessary to the description. Elimination of any or all of them would make the thought obscure.

"He held his red and blue, red-visored baseball cap in his chubby, stubby, fat, short-fingered hands. His big, blue, wide, unblinking eyes looked up at the tall, long-legged, muscular figure towering over him." Cross out all the unnecessary junk. It does not add to the description. It does not improve the picture. "He held his red-visored baseball cap in his chubby hands. His unblinking eyes looked up at the figure towering over him."

Adverbs

Another place to look for words that are destroying your simple and direct writing is in front of the adjectives and verbs, where the adverbs hang out.

"It was a very hot day with scarcely any movement. A boy and his dog wandered slowly, listlessly and effortlessly through the slightly grimy street. The clearly shimmering heat really left very little energy in the traditionally malnourished inhabitants of that unusually but not atypically poor hamlet." Try it this way: "It was so hot there was scarcely any movement. A boy and his dog wandered through the grimy street. The heat left little energy in the malnourished inhabitants of the poor hamlet."

Adverbs are like adjectives. They have their place in that they further describe verbs and adjectives. Make sure you use them only for that. Use both adjectives and adverbs when the thought cannot stand without them, when they are genuinely contributing to what you are saying. When in doubt, cross them out.

Nouns and verbs in sequences

Nouns and verbs are usually necessary. They do not tend to be the main culprits in overwriting. They offend principally when they are used in sequences. For instance: "Clerical workers, typists, filing clerks, and stenographers should not be allowed to work overtime and stay late because overtime contributes to and aids overspending and waste on salaries and pay." Say: "Clerical workers should not be allowed to work overtime because overtime contributes to over-spending on salaries."

Introductory, temporizing and explanatory words

We use introductory, temporizing, and explanatory words or phrases in speech constantly to allow us time to think. We say, "Well, I guess we could do that," or "Let's see now, somehow there must be a way to, well, remove the ladder without, maybe, scratching the wall."

In writing, such phrases are unnecessary. The assumption is that you have time to think before you write. There should be no stalling for thoughts when you are writing. Say it simply and directly: "I could do that," or "There must be a way to remove the ladder without scratching the wall."

Unnecessary repetition

When you are speaking, your listeners may, for one reason or another, miss what you said. You may have to repeat it to be sure they understood. Not so in writing. If a reader misses what you say, he can always go back and reread it. Repetition serves a different purpose in writing. It is used for emphasis. It is a specific tool to accomplish specific goals, namely the stressing of particular points for emphasis and clarity.

Often repetition in a slightly different manner is advantageous to clarify a thought. We have no quarrel with that.

What we do object to is the repetition of thoughts that

need no particular emphasis. "We went to the show in the early afternoon. The matinee started at 2 o'clock and we had to hurry to get there on time. We arrived just as the curtain was going up on the afternoon performance."

Such sequences are all too common. The poor writer is trying so hard to be absolutely clear about what happened that he cannot spot what he is doing wrong. He is sacrificing simplicity for clarity. But he need not give up one for the other. The two go together. Keep it simple *and* clear: "We arrived just as the curtain was going up on the 2 o'clock matinee."

Not enough to say

Perhaps the principal cause of overwriting, that is, using too many words to express yourself, is the fear of not having enough to say. In so many writing contexts, it seems as if the length of the work is dictated by outside circumstances. The classic case is the student who must write to order for a teacher. "Give me a composition of 500 words on the meaning of life." The teacher is dictating both the subject and the length. The immediate reaction of the student is fear that he does not have that much to say. So right from the opening sentence he starts counting words and putting in as many as he can think of. And he loves to say "at this point in time," when he means "now." Five words are better than one.

The problem occurs in more subtle form in most writing situations. When you start a letter to family, you try to fill one page at least. The size of your stationery is dictating the length. An editor asks for no more than three pages. A minister knows he must write six pages if his sermon is to last a half hour. In memos at work, you are not sure you have made your case strongly enough, so you start repeating.

The problem is largely a bogus one. It is a fear often

groundless. Most professional writers have the exact opposite experience. They write too much. They can't say all they have to say within the limits imposed upon them. Ask a reporter for a page and a half and he will give you two. Ask him for three if you want four. Good writers usually find they have to cut back on content because even with close-to-the-bone writing, they have too much to say.

Why this difference? Why do poor writers think they have too little to say and thus have to flesh out their writing, while good writers have so much to say they concentrate on saying it succinctly?

The professional writers have learned a simple trick: Flesh out the thought, not the expression of it.

They read, they research, they probe, until they have so many thoughts on the subject they cannot possibly put them all into writing. When they sit at their typewriters, they are trying to get so many ideas into the writing that they pare each one to the essential. The result is that they are good writers. Their writing is simple and direct. That is why they succeed. But their writing is simple and direct because they can afford to make it so.

Flesh out the thought, not the expression of it.

That simple trick, fleshing out the thought, is one that every writer, good or bad, can use. Why do bad writers never seem to do it? Maybe it is the other way around. Maybe those who do not do it are invariably bad writers.

At any rate, if you learn to depend on collecting an over-supply of ideas on any subject you tackle in writing, you will quickly lose your fear of not having enough to say. With it you will lose the need for counting words and for overwriting. You will find yourself reverting to simple, direct, effective writing.

When you do not have enought to say on a subject, spend a little time in the library. Read up on it. Don't blame the teacher or editor who assigned it.

Simple words

The tendency to use longer words in writing than in speaking is almost universal these days. Evidently the pretense at scholarship is more important to the writer than the loss of clarity. Presumably the writer feels he will be taken more seriously if he dresses what he says in tuxedos and gowns than if he uses jeans and shorts. He is seeking acceptance and belief through word choice rather than through the truth and strength of his ideas. Or—one step further—he may be disguising in the complexities of vocabulary his own lack of security in what he is saying.

Learn to depend on the accuracy of your ideas and the clarity of your expression, rather than on the number of letters in the words you use. There is nothing wrong with using big words and phrases if they best express the idea. Sometimes accuracy requires it. But big words should never be for show or as a smokescreen around fuzzy thinking.

Whenever possible, turn in all that sesquipedalian glossolalia for simple, direct statements. Don't say the cowboy expectorated when he spat his tobacco juice. Don't report the number of domiciles and housing units when your boss wants to know how many homes there are. Why maintain periodic verbal contact when you can keep in touch by phone? And for goodness sakes, Howard, did he really experience momentary uncustomary manual disability, or did he just plain drop the ball?

Short and clear sentences

Long, convoluted sentences are confusing. By the time you reach the verb, you have forgotten the subject. If the sentence is long enough, it can mean anything or nothing. Perhaps that is why bureaucrats and politicians seem to love long sentences.

Your thoughts have a natural flow, a rhythm to them. That flow should dictate the length of the sentence. In speech, the flow of your thoughts is broken into concise and manageable units by the need for breath. You run out of air and have to pause. Your mind operates in synchronization with your lungs.

No pen company, however, has yet produced a pen that only writes in short, rhythmic spurts. Writers don't have to pause. And often writers don't.

One of the problems with brevity in writing is that it is a rule laden with exceptions. Top writers use long, multi-phrased sentences with ease. They have learned to do so without sacrificing thought. Less skillful writers see this and decide to imitate. Not being masters, they soon become enmeshed in a tangled web of word ropes. Someday, you may be able to write long, effective sentences. When you reach that stage, you will know you are there by your understanding of exactly what you are doing. You are nowhere near that plateau now.

Check yourself. You will probably find you do not pause for breath often enough. You probably tend to include too much in an individual sentence. If your sentences are routinely long, try breaking them up. You will be surprised how much clearer they become. "The northeast sales district, which consists of more than 2,000 clients each of whom must be contacted twice each quarter according to company policy, but which spreads across hundreds of miles of roads that are often narrow, is too much for two salesmen to handle by car, which is why I recommend either adding a couple more salesmen or allowing more air travel, at least between points readily accessible to airplanes." Perfectly true. But not effective. "The northeast sales district consists of 2,000 clients. They are spread over hundreds of miles; in towns often accessible only by narrow roads. Yet company policy dictates that each client must be visited twice a quarter. It is an impossible situation.

Could two more salesmen be added to that district? Or could more air travel be allowed between points readily accessible to airplanes?"

So often, clarity is in inverse ratio to the length of the sentence. We stress the need for short sentences because the common fault of inexperienced writers is long sentences. We mentioned earlier, however, that such a rule is riddled with exceptions. Long sentences are not by nature poor sentences or poor writing. They are just more dangerous to attempt, much harder to use without sacrificing clarity.

At the same time, the rhythm of your thoughts—which we also alluded to earlier—can and should dictate the length of your sentences. In brief, short sentences are hard-hitting, exciting, emphatic. They portray action. Long sentences set moods, reflect serenity, leisure, complacency.

A practical rule is: Let your thought dictate the length of your sentences; but when the thought is not dictating a specific length, keep them short.

"He raised his gun. I dove. There were trees to my left. I rolled. I ran. A shot sounded behind me. I heard running footsteps behind me. The trees loomed up. I dove behind the nearest one. The footsteps stopped. He wasn't coming in here after me. Then I saw why. Four Dobermans, teeth bared, were silently stalking me through the trees."

Short sentences portray action, excitement, urgency.

"I lay back in the grass and let the sensations flow over me. The breeze in the high meadow had just a nip of chill to it, a harbinger of cool, autumn nights to be followed inevitably by deep, snowy winter. The swallows circling overhead, silhouetted against fluffy clouds, had no thought of snow yet. They were devoting their full attention to catching the next insect, dipping and sailing, their wings flashing golden in the lowering sun. Why can't I lie here forever, soaking in the sun and the pure air, watching the distant peaks change color, and living with the simple, eternal cares of the village women who are cutting hay and feeding husks to cattle that live on the ground floor of their steep-roofed houses?

"Then I thought of Agnes. And Malcolm. A shiver moved up from the small of my back. I sat up. I had to do something."

Long sentences portray contentment, leisure, peace. Notice how the mood is interrupted as much by the short sentences as by a change in thought.

Stick to short sentences unless you are intentionally trying to set a flowing, reassuring, complacent mood.

Fuzzy thinking

Nothing destroys clarity in writing as quickly as fuzzy thinking by the writer. It is inevitable. If you are not sure what you are trying to say, you cannot state it clearly. That is why we spent so much time in the first part of this book on controlling ideas and organization. We were trying to establish clear thoughts from which to write.

Fuzzy thinking can arise at any point in a piece of writing despite effective controlling ideas and clear organization.

When these pockets of confusion interrupt the flow of your ideas, there is no other treatment possible except to straighten out your thinking.

You will recognize these minor problems, if you are looking for them, by a change in the rhythm of your work. You will bog down. You will begin to write too much, explain too much. You will stumble, grope for words, wonder what to say next. You will find yourself drifting from your controlling idea.

To analyze a trouble spot, go back to basics. Is the thought you are trying to express valid? Does it effectively support the controlling idea? Consider it briefly as a small controlling idea of its own. Can you express it as a controlling idea? How would you support that controlling idea? What makes it valid and to the point? If the problem is nagging enough, actually write down a small outline of the paragraph in question.

Almost always, if you do this, you will find you have become caught up in some digression that is not really to the point of your controlling idea. Most of the time, fuzzy thinking is simply thinking that is not pertinent to what you are trying to accomplish with the writing.

Why do we include this section under brevity and directness, instead of under the controlling idea? Because when your thinking is fuzzy you are likely to become wordy. You will surely lose emphasis. You will wander off and you will come back to the point from the wrong angle. Your problems will express themselves in writing that is neither brief nor direct.

Only after straightening out your thinking can you write that paragraph easily and forcefully, with brevity and directness.

Specialized jargon

Always keep your audience in mind. It is not enough that you know the meaning of the words you use. That is taken for granted. Your audience must also understand them. When you are writing for a specialized group, engineers, union members, orthodontists, or lepidopterists, you certainly should not hesitate to use the vocabulary of the trade. If you are writing in a business context, you can presume considerable understanding of the technical terms of that business. And you can use them effectively.

Be careful whenever crossing disciplines. And be careful about using specialized terms to a general audience. This is the mistake so many bureaucrats, professors, and research scientists make. They become so involved in their sphere of reference that they often cannot—even when they want to and are trying to—shift back into common English. Doctors can be extremely annoying when they try to tell you in medical terms what is wrong with you. If they said you had a virus, a pinched nerve, or a broken leg, you would understand. Instead, they use the technical terms and make you think you are dying of some dread disease. They speak of contusions and abrasions when you have bruises and cuts.

We once witnessed a computer expert telling a client again and again that a modum coupler would make remote operations completely transparent. Since a large contract was at stake, the client kept trying to clarify the point. The expert simply could not put it into plain English. Finally the client asked, "Do you mean with this little switch I can put terminals miles away from the central office and my people can still use the computer just as easily as if they were sitting right next to it?" "Yes," said the expert. "How many times do I have to tell you?"

If you are engaged in publishing directives, studies, or reports of any kind, do the world a big favor and write them in the same kind of English you use at home, not the kind of bureaucrat-ese, computer-ese, research-ese or any other ese-y way out that renders what you are doing ineffective and unintelligible. You can still be accurate. The English language is diverse enough to handle it.

If you must employ special terms for general readership, define and explain them clearly the first time you use them. The next few times, give a quick refresher summary of the meaning. If our computer expert had explained two terms, modum coupler and transparent, in the meaning he was giving them, he could have saved himself lots of time and trouble.

Slang

Slang is a relative of jargon. While jargon refers to a special discipline or business, slang refers to the vocabulary and usage of a particular social class, age group or region. Slang is colorful; it is apt; it is descriptive; it is usually to the point. Slang can convey meaning as accurately as any words in the English language.

The problem with slang is its transience. It comes into and disappears from the language so quickly that it immediately dates the writing. Slang quickly gives writing an obsolete character.

A few years ago, the thrust into space gave us a whole new set of words. So did the Watergate hearings, the hippie movement, and the protests of the late sixties. These quickly and inevitably faded, lost their immediacy and appeal, and took their rightful place with the lost slang of the thirties and forties. "A-OK," "splashdown," "expletive deleted," "no longer operative," "get it together," "flower power," and "let it all hang out" sound as quaint today as "swell," "dilly," and "spooning."

The second danger in using slang is that not all of your audience may understand it or give it the same meaning you do. Slang meanings develop quickly, are tied to a specific social setting, and quickly fade. If you hope what you are writing will cross out of the narrow limit of time and space, the slang will probably take on a completely different and often unintelligible character to your readers. And that you cannot afford. You are working too hard on effective writing, on directness and clarity, to allow yourself to fall into the traps set by social context. Stick to proven, accepted, tested words and your writing will be accurate, accepted, and effective.

Style

One last point remains to be made under simplicity and directness. That concerns the question of style.

We will take up style and its ramifications at some length in Chapter Seven. For now, we would like to give a word of warning about the connection between style and directness.

The desire for one's own style is the most common excuse for using 24-karat words in two-bit situations. In teaching and editing, we ask our writers again and again why they used the words and sentences they did. They usually first claim it is their natural style, then admit it is the style they think they should have. It is neither. Style is not something you can simply put on. It can never be phony. It is a natural quality. The achievement of style can only be accomplished by passing through the narrow door of clarity. Style builds upon and depends upon direct, clear, effective writing, not the other way around.

You will never develop an effective style by sacrificing clarity, directness or naturalness—unless the individual trait you want to characterize your style, become your trademark, is pomposity or pretentiousness. More on this subject later.

CHAPTER SIX

Some Common Problems

Most aspiring writers could greatly improve their efforts by coming to grips with a few basic facts about the effective use of the English language as a means of communication. You are probably making some errors that are not particularly hard to correct. You are probably not even aware how much they are hurting your writing.

In this chapter, we are going to discuss briefly some of the most common and most easily corrected writing mistakes.

The right word

It seems elementary that a writer should use the proper word to express himself in all circumstances. In practice, writers often do not. In many cases it is a question of a limited vocabulary. In many others, it is sloppiness or carelessness. In some few cases, it results from a mental block. Whatever the cause, it can be easily cured.

People get into the habit of expressing themselves through a limited vocabulary. They know thousands of words they never use in speech. Their limited vocabulary seems to work satisfactorily in speech, when the tone of voice, gestures, subsequent explanations, all aid the task of communicating. In writing, inaccuracy will not be tolerated, even by a reader who would not object in a spoken context. In writing, "what I mean, man, is . . ." and "you know, like . . ." and "you see, . . ." all sound foolish. You are supposed to make the effort to say it right the first time. You are expected to take one shot at it. If that shot is off the mark in a rough draft, you can scratch it out and try again. In the final writing, however, it has to be right.

Nothing but the right word is acceptable in writing.

The right meaning

Make sure the word means what you mean. You are not the slave of vocabulary. It is the other way around. Vocabulary is your tool for expressing yourself. You strive for the right meaning only because that right meaning will enable you to express yourself, to communicate, effectively. Yet it is so easy, so common—and so damaging—to use a word in the wrong context, to miss the meaning. The important thing is that you understand what you want to say and that you use words that say what you want.

It is surprising how many words that you hear misused in conversation are also misused on television. Presumably those who speak on television are the best communicators in the country. It is hard to say whether announcers misuse words because they are speaking the language of their audience, or ordinary citizens misuse them because they hear them misused on television. "Good" is an adjective. It modifies nouns. "Well" is an adverb. It modifies verbs and adjectives. Simple. Yet how often you hear, "He didn't do so good!" "Fewer" measures separate items; "less" measures quantity. You have fewer marbles in a jar, but less water in a jar. So you never have less than five trees on your lawn. You have fewer. And a beer never can have less calories. We know a man who likes to say, "Let's digress on that subject for a few minutes." And we usually do digress. What he means, though, is "Let's discuss that subject." "Let's get rid of all this nitty-gritty and deal with the essentials." "Nitty-gritty," of course, means the essentials, not the details. "That's for the hoi polloi, not for us ordinary people." "Hoi polloi" means ordinary people. "I can't convince him to come along." "Convince" refers only to ideas, as in "I can't convince him the world is round." "Persuade" refers to talking into action, as in "I can't persuade him to come along."

There are infinite variations that can lead to wrong meaning. That is the glory of the language. Those infinite variations also allow us to express an infinite range of ideas. Despite the variations, it is not only possible, it is almost always easy to get the meaning right.

If you happen to be unsure, use a dictionary. It is designed specifically for checking the meanings of words that you are unsure of. Getting the meaning right is the only way to make words work effectively for you.

Close is not good enough

So often in writing, the word you want simply does not come to mind. You know it is there; you know it is a common word you use all the time; but you sit at your typewriter and cannot think of it. It is one of the most frustrating experiences in writing. It happens to all writers.

Don't let it go. That is the danger. You might have to go on with the writing, but put a mark on your paper at the point to remind yourself that you have a slightly wrong word in as a substitute for the correct one. Sometimes, when you return to it you can think of the word you wanted. Often the mental block that keeps you from thinking of it is only temporary. So it often pays to go on.

It never pays, though, to consider the work complete, to give the memo to your boss, the promotional letter to your client, the paper to your teacher, the note to your boyfriend, before you find and insert the proper word.

Accuracy of expression is the essence of accuracy of communication. If you do not say what you mean, you cannot expect the reader to understand what you are trying to communicate.

What happens in those cases where the proper word does not come to you later? There is a tool used by all writers, serious or casual, to help them come up with the appropriate word. It is called a thesaurus, and even (especially?) the most casual writer should have one handy when he is writing. A thesaurus is a book, similar to a dictionary, which collects words by meaning instead of alphabetically. In a thesaurus, all words of similar meaning are lumped together. When you can think of a word that is close to what you mean, find that word in a thesaurus and you will find listed with it all the words that have meanings close to the word you have looked up. So if you have used a word that is not quite right in meaning, the perfect word should be listed with it in the thesaurus. A perfectly adequate paperback thesaurus costs only a few dollars and will earn its price over and over again. You will find it easy to use and the perfect answer for finding the right word.

Word size

It is a common mistake, as we have indicated elsewhere, for writers to try to use big, formal, pretentious words in writing that they would never think of using in speech. There is nothing wrong with doing so, in itself. The problem is that such big words usually have slightly different meanings from the smaller ones they replace. And the writer sacrifices the variation in meaning. The reader, who usually knows what he should have said, is not at all sympathetic. So the writer, attempting to looked cultured, usually looks ridiculous instead.

Another problem with choosing the right word is that ordinary spoken words are often imprecise in meaning. Words that are used commonly often develop wide, generic meanings. The reader may visualize the wrong one. House, run, fat, good, road, friend, tree, say, work, such words cover a wide range of meanings and experiences. Beware of them. How much more meaningful are the slightly less common chalet, gallop, plump, virtuous, lane, acquaintance, maple, explain, function. Killing and murder are not always the same. A backhoe and a crane are not the same. A valley and a ravine are different.

The point is: don't use a word because it sounds impressive, long or short, common or uncommon; use the word because it is accurate. Use it because it conveys to the reader exactly what you want it to.

Connotations and denotations

Speaking of using the precise word, connotation and denotation are not the same. Denotation is the meaning of the word. Connotation is the aura of intangible impressions that surrounds it. It is what you think of when you see the word, which may or may not be what it means. The meaning of skinny and thin is the same. In reference to people, both words denote one who does not carry excessive weight. The connotation of the words is completely different. Being thin is complimentary, good form, proper, and to be desired according to the standards of our society. Being skinny carries negative connotations of ill health, lack of proper nutrition, even slyness or furtiveness.

One is reminded of an article said to have appeared in a Russian newspaper a number of years ago after a head-to-head track meet between the U.S.A. and the Soviet Union. The U.S.A. won the two-team meet by a wide margin. The headline in the Russian newspaper the next day is reported to have read: "Russia finishes second in big track meet; U.S.A. ends up next to last." The denotation is absolutely correct. But watch out for those connotations.

What is the difference between "concerned about quality" and "picky?" The same house can be quaint and rundown. The same man can be determined and stubborn.

Connotations bring us face to face with euphemisms. A euphemism is a polite word used for a blunt, crude, or unacceptable one. We have nothing against euphemisms. We don't happen to believe that four-letter accuracy is a sign of either good writing or realism. Euphemisms soften unpleasant or indelicate truths. In euphemisms, the denotation is the same, but the connotation is much gentler. Why do women perspire while men sweat? Because the connotation is so much more delicate. An undertaker speaks of a man passing away because he fears the relatives cannot face the fact that the man died. A football player is released by the team, never fired. Fair enough. Soften the blow for normal social politeness.

Euphemisms can be carried to extremes, obviously, and doing so would not be good writing. A plumber is not a sanitation engineer. A paramedic is not a doctor. The radio or TV weatherman is not a meteorologist. He has no degree in meteorology.

You need not always be blunt. The softer connotation may be the one you are looking for. Most of the time it probably is. If you are aware of the connotations as well as the denotations of words, you will be able to choose the proper word for the circumstances in which you are writing. After all, perspire does mean (denote) the same thing as sweat.

Clichés

Many inexperienced writers derive confidence from using phrases someone else has thought up for them. They stay within the safe boundaries of thoughts that have been expressed often before. The most perfect way of expressing a thought is seized upon by many people, used again and again, until through overwork it loses its freshness, meaning, and impact. When it reaches that stage, it is called a cliché.

Once in a blue moon. As smooth as silk. Quick as a wink. Snug as a bug in a rug. Cute as a kitten. Dirty as a pig; meek as a lamb; faithful as a dog; sly as a fox.

Clichés generally add nothing to writing. Since they have become meaningless, they bog down writing and make it boring. They waste words.

Avoid clichés like the plague. "Like the plague" is a cliché. At one time, it was clever and meaningful. Now it is just filler. So avoid clichés at all costs. "At all costs" is also a cliché. So what do you say? How do you avoid the ever-present cliché? How about simply "avoid clichés?" Direct, clear, to the point. The way your writing should be. If you feel you must try to dress up the thought in a colorful expression, at least try to make it something fresh and meaningful. Avoid clichés as if they were homework? Avoid clichés like carcinogens? Avoid clichés like the tax collector? More on such figures of speech in Chapter Eight. For now, avoid clichés.

Active vocabulary

This tip does not apply to a specific piece of writing. It suggests a basic tool that can have an immense effect on your writing over the long haul. To understand its value, it is necessary to have a basic understanding of how the mind deals with language.

In your mind, you actually have two separate vocabularies, two distinct sets of words with which you deal.

The first set of words is the set you use every day in speech, thought, and writing. It is made up of the ordinary words you use. It is called your active vocabulary, because you actively use the words in it when you are trying to express yourself.

You also have a second vocabulary called the passive vocabulary. This is made up of words whose meaning you understand when you hear or see them, but words which you simply do not use in your normal speech or writing. It is called passive because it just sits there, waiting for the word to strike your senses from outside. It aids your understanding, but it is not part of your vocabulary when you are expressing your thoughts.

This passive vocabulary is many times larger than the active. You know the meanings of all those words, know how to use them. You are just not in the habit of doing so. How long since you have used any of these words: contrive, goblet, tarmac, residual, canister, perceive, copious, verandah, haughty, opaque, unseemly? Yet they are common words whose usage you are familiar with.

One of the easiest ways to increase your writing accuracy is to increase your active vocabulary. The more words you have available to you, the more accurate you will be. Yet learning new words is often a tedious process. Learning to transfer words you already know from your passive to your active vocabulary is a much simpler and more effective way of increasing dramatically your writing vocabulary.

There are many ways to transfer those words. The simplest way is to make a note of them as they reach your ear from outside. In substance, say to yourself, "That is a word I could be using. I know what it means; I just never think to use it." And make yourself a mental note to use it the next time you get the opportunity. That may be all it takes to implant it in your active memory. Certainly, forcing yourself to use it a couple of times will do so. Then, but only then, will it be at your disposal as a writer.

Each individual word you bring from passive to active vocabulary will not make much difference. But if you keep doing it, you will find you are expressing yourself more accurately and more clearly all the time.

Beginnings and endings

There are two parts of a written work that are more important than any others. They are the beginning and the ending.

When a reader starts to read, he is full of anticipation. By the very action of picking up what you have written, he is disposing himself to understand and appreciate what you are communicating. That mood, which is the best you could hope for in a reader, may not last for long. It may last only a few words if your writing is not stimulating. You must make the most of it. It is up to you, the writer, to seize upon that opportunity and give the reader such powerful openers that he will not put the writing back down. You must grab his interest and stimulate it. You must lure him into your writing.

Puzzle your readers with a paradox, pique their curiosity with a question, amuse them with an anecdote, astound them with an obscure fact or a mind-boggling statistic, or, perhaps most effective of all, get them emotionally involved with someone they can identify with. If you do, they are almost certain to continue reading.

People are naturally interested in people. Writers should know this. They should hook their readers with stories about Mrs. Jones who earned a college degree at age 81; or Mr. and Mrs. Smith who cannot afford to feed their five children and heat their drafty Victorian house at the same time; or Mr. Brown who manages to run a plumbing business, do all the housework, and raise two preschool daughters. Reporters, feature and magazine writers have learned this lesson well and use such material routinely. It never wears out. It is always effective. After such openers, they gently lead their readers into a discussion of the widening interests of the elderly, the effects of rising fuel costs on low-income families, or the growing tendency to award custody of small children to fathers in divorce cases. A personalized opener is difficult to resist because it combines specificity with emotional appeal. Although it might not work in a business memo, it works consistently in most kinds of writing including articles and student papers. It can even enliven dry research papers.

You must start by giving your reader reasons for continuing and for paying attention.

The other important part of a work is the ending. It is your last shot at the reader. You must drive home the point, the controlling idea. You will not get another chance. But with the ending, you are doing a far different thing from what you wanted at the beginning. You do not want your readers to continue reading; you want them to leave impressed with what you had to say.

The most common problem with ending is not knowing when to. Inexperienced writers tend to go on too long. Speak your piece; then hold your peace. Don't restate, restate, and restate. Don't summarize if you have only written a few pages. The material has not had time to slip away from the reader, so a summary is not only unnecessary, it is annoying. Summaries are for long works.

If you are using the climactic aproach to writing, your last statements should be your most forceful. Fire those howitzers, then sit tight. Don't soften the landing or water down the effect.

Effective beginnings and endings do not vary as much as might be supposed with different kinds of writing. In business, no matter whether you are trying to sell your boss, your fellow department heads, or your employees, whether you are buying or selling, you will usually be most effective if you concentrate on stirring interest with your beginning and driving home your main point with your ending.

Beginning: "Wouldn't it be convenient if ore purification could be accomplished without the heat from the furnace escaping into the work area? . . ."

Ending: ". . . This air shield would not only direct the excess heat away from the work area; it would use that heat to perform preliminary melting and separating."

The beginning draws you in and the ending drives the point home.

"Replacing broken windows in this building cost $12,000 last year, and four-fifths of those windows were broken from the inside. . . . The wire-center glass panels are not only shatterproof; they are also burglarproof. They pay for themselves many times over in a short time."

"Dear Mom,

I'm dropping engineering because my math marks are so low . . . that is why I am following my counselor's advice and switching to the major I am most qualified for psychologically—law."

"Twenty hot-air balloons will bring 100 clowns to the parking lot in front of city hall, where they will be greeted by the chief of police. . . . But in order for us, the Lions, to successfully carry out these ambitious festival plans, every member of this club must do his part."

Transitions

A transition in writing is that point at which you shift from one thought to another. You may make a transition between sentences or between paragraphs. You may go a number of sentences or paragraphs without making a transition.

Whenever you face a transition, though, you are facing a potential trouble spot, a spot at which you could give your reader problems. The reader must be led smoothly and coherently from one thought to the next.

There are two normally accepted ways of making transitions smooth and clear: repetition of key words and use of transitional words. They are not the only ways to accomplish a transition. In fact, they may not be the best. Great writers often accomplish transitions without any artificial aids at all. Most writers, though, lean on both of these methods, now one, now the other.

Repetition

If you switch gears too quickly, they will grind on the reader. He will not be sure what is happening. So whenever possible, establish a connection between the previous passage and the one to come. The best way to establish this connection is by repeating.

There are many things you can repeat to establish a smooth transition. The easiest is to repeat key words. "Recession is unavoidable because of the tight interest rates. Recession is even more unavoidable because of the uneven balance of payments." The repetition of "recession is unavoidable" accomplishes the transition in thought smoothly. Sometimes you do not repeat words. Instead you can repeat a grammatical or structural pattern. "Everyone acknowledges that consumerism is destructive of natural resources. Few recognize how insidiously it damages the national moral fiber." No words are repeated, but the structural pattern of "Everyone acknowledges" is repeated in "Few recognize" and the transition is clear.

A third way of accomplishing a transition through use of repetition is by summarizing what has come before as a lead into a new thought. "Although *The House of the Seven Gables* is clearly allegorical, it could also be considered biographical." "Even if we put the recommended $20,000 into the new desks, the faulty air conditioner cannot be ignored."

Connecting words

Connecting words are just what the name says, words that do not add meaning but function to draw together thoughts during a transition. These are pretty much common words used automatically in attempts at communication. And, but, however, although, furthermore, despite, because, etc. are among the most common. These connecting words can be divided into categories depending upon what is to be accomplished. Here are a few common categories and some connecting words for transitions of that kind.

When you want to develop the same thought some more, use furthermore, in addition, secondly (thirdly or fourthly), besides, likewise, also.

To indicate the change to a different or opposing point of view, use but, however, nevertheless, instead, on the other hand, still, yet.

To indicate a result or conclusion from what has come before, use therefore, accordingly, thus, as a result, consequently.

To indicate a change in time, or the absence of a change in time, say meanwhile, later, at the same time, afterwards, soon.

You get the idea. If you are having trouble making a transition, call upon connecting words.

The use of connecting words presents a danger of which you should be aware. Connecting words tend to become filler words. You will tend to use them to flesh out the writing, as the written equivalent of a pause or the clearing of the throat. As we indicated before, such things have their place in speech which is spontaneous, but not in writing, which is a studied and calculated process.

Make sure the connecting words are necessary. Make sure they are fulfilling their purpose, which is to bind together clearly a preceding and following thought. Try leaving the connecting word out whenever possible. If the text reads as clearly without it, leave it out.

CHAPTER SEVEN

Style and Tone

Definition of style

Style is the way a thought, a controlling idea, is expressed. It is what results from the linguistic and grammatical choices of the writer.

Each word, each sentence the writer puts down on paper is an arbitrary choice. The writer picks a specific word out of the many he could use. He picks ten specific words and strings them together in a specific order. This arbitrary choice of words and the arbitrary way in which they are strung together produce an effect on the reader. They trigger certain mental and emotional reactions in the reader. They summon up images in the mind of the reader. If the writing is good, what the reader thinks, what he understands from the writing, will be close to what the writer wanted him to understand.

You are leaving a note to your sister to stay at home until your mother returns from the store. You can do it many ways.

"Mother is at the store. Please wait for her to return home before you leave."

"Stay home till Ma gets back."

"Would you please await the return of your mother before leaving the house?"

"Remain a moment longer at the family residence so that your mother's arrival precedes your departure."

"You better not leave before Mom gets home, or you're in big trouble!"

Each example says substantially the same thing. Each is understandable. but each is in a different style. And each evokes a slightly different image in the reader.

Style, to put it another way then, is the individual and personal way in which a writer expresses his thoughts.

**Relation to content and
effectiveness**

Content is what you say. Effectiveness is how accurately and forcefully the reader grasps what you are saying. Style is how you say it.

In any writing, the three are inextricably intertwined. The three, in fact, make up the essential elements of any piece of writing.

Of the three, style is the least important. It is secondary to the other two, both of which are indispensable. You cannot be using poor style if you express your thought effectively.

Your style cannot be good if your thought is not expressed effectively.

In this book we dealt first with content. We talked about what you want to say, how you develop your controlling ideas so they can be expressed effectively, how you clarify and order your thoughts on a subject.

Beginning with Chapter Four, we switched the concentration to methods of expressing your thought effectively on paper.

Now we are ready to take up the style in which you as an individual express those ideas effectively.

Basic components of style

Because of the complexity and subtlety of language, the writer has infinite variables at his disposal when he sits down to write. That is why no two writers ever express themselves in exactly the same way, even though they may be writing on the same topic. No matter how many people write on love or the economy, all will write something different, express themselves somewhat differently (unless, of course, one is plagiarizing from another).

The infinite variation, however, can be broken down into a few categories. Here we will limit ourselves to four important ones and we will try to show how these categories affect style.

Diction

Diction is the choice of words with which we express ourselves. At first glance, it might seem there is only one word to describe each object, each action, each idea in our mind. We are either eating or we are not. That object is a hill or it is not. Not so. Even with such obvious objects and actions we have a wide variety of words to describe them. And each word gives the description a slightly different flavor. We could be dining, picnicking, supping, gulping our food, munching, nibbling, or gnawing. That object could be a mountain, a ski slope, a knoll, a ridge, a mound, a butte, a crag, or a rise.

Word choice adds flavor to what you write. The pattern you use in choosing words is a basic element in your style. What you are trying to accomplish, what effect you are shooting for, will usually dictate your word choice. Obviously, you have to choose words that create the effect you want.

Within diction (or word choice) words are usually divided up by their roots. By that we mean by the language from which they came originally. The English language is made up of elements from many languages. The two principal languages from which English is formed are Latin and Anglo-Saxon. How that happened is not important to us here. What is important is that Latin and Anglo-Saxon words usually carry different connotations and therefore make different styles available to the writer.

Latin words tend to be long and smooth, polysyllabic. They often convey scholarship, polish, distinction. Anglo-Saxon words tend to be short and sharp. They convey immediacy, specificity, bluntness. "Receive" has a Latin root. So does "obtain." "Get" and "take" come from the Anglo-Saxon. The following are Latinate words: significance, location, victorious, persevering, manufacture. Here are similar Anglo-Saxon words: meaning, spot, winning, stubborn, make. In Latinate English you might say, "Conscription is a necessary precursor to the execution of extensive military operations." The same thing in Anglo-Saxon English would be: "If there's going to be a war, there will have to be a draft."

Neither is more correct. It depends on what you are trying to accomplish. You do not even have to know the root of a word to use it for stylistic purposes. To make words contribute to your style, however, you do have to be aware of the image different words will convey to the reader. You have to use diction carefully and precisely.

Syntax

Syntax means the way in which words are strung together to form phrases and sentences. The basic syntactical distinction is between simple and complex. Simple sentences are those that consist of only one subject-verb-object combination. They do not have subordinate (dependent) clauses. Complex sentences are those consisting of more than one set of subjects and verbs. They often have many phrases and clauses.

"The school bus stopped to pick up two girls. The driver did not see a small boy come out of the house next door. The boy stepped into the street without looking. The driver started the bus. The bus hit the boy," Simple syntax.

"After the school bus had stopped to pick up two girls, as it was starting up again, the driver didn't see a small boy who, having come out of the house next door, stepped into the street without looking, and was hit by the bus." Complex sentence. Notice that it says the same thing.

Again, either is correct. Longer, more complex sentences tend to set a relaxed, smooth, unemotional pace. Simple, short sentences tend to be fast-paced, action-packed, dramatic. It depends what you are trying to accomplish with your style.

Modifiers

Modifiers are descriptive words attached to the main words to further clarify the meaning. They contribute to style in two ways.

First, the choice of modifiers gives you more opportunities to set style and mood through diction. We have already dealt with how diction affects style. A pink suit conveys a much different image from a pinstriped suit. "He gave him a rap across the back of the head" is a lot different from, "He gave him a friendly rap across the back of the head." Adjectives and adverbs are effective ways to develop style through diction.

You can also vary your style by using many or few modifiers. "The wagon rolled down the hill." No modifiers. Just a simple statement of what happened. "The creaking, old, four-wheeled hay wagon, loaded with aluminum cans filled with fresh milk, rolled out of control down the side of the hill, picking up speed as it went." Lots of modifiers. They explain much more, make the picture clearer. They also change the writing style greatly.

In general, the more modifiers, the more complete the information given, but the slower the pace. The writer must make the decision on how many modifiers are necessary to portray accurately what he wants to say. The result of that decision will be a major part of his style.

Treatment

Treatment of subject matter can mean almost anything. Here we want to limit the phrase to a very specific usage. We mean by it the directness of the approach. You can be direct or evasive, blunt or polite, in your approach to what you write. "Pay up or I'll break your arm." Direct. "Abhorrent though a physical approach to the problem may be to both our natures, it is becoming apparent that no pressure short of that has accomplished my goal, which is the payment by you of your overdue debt." Indirect.

Again, circumstances dictate how direct and blunt you want to be with your writing. How direct you are in turn contributes greatly to your writing style.

Reflecting your personality

Although style is a tool for effective expression of your thought, there can be no denying that ultimately and secondarily style also reflects your personality. No matter how neutral you try to be, the words you choose, the sentence structure you use will be individualistic and will reveal aspects of your personality. This is why all writing, not only autobiographical writing, is an act of self-revelation. It cannot be avoided. The ego is always a part of writing. As a result, writing, and especially the editing or correction of writing, is often a painful process. When an editor changes a word or a chapter of your writing, he is striking right at your personality itself.

The very fact that writing is an act of self-revelation can be utilized to inspire good writing. If you remember that your personality is reflected in what you write, you will strive to write well. If you write clearly, directly, and effectively, you are reflecting your own mind. If you write passionately, you are reflecting a warm, emotional disposition. Harnessing your psyche in your writing, using it to provide power for your writing, is one of the keys to truly effective writing.

How can you or anyone harness the psyche for powerful writing? It is not as difficult as it sounds. The concept to remember is authenticity. Let yourself go. Be yourself. Say what you think how you think it. What is clearest to you will surely be clearest to your readers. What impresses you will also usually impress your reader.

What we are saying here is really what we have been saying all along. Aim for clarity, directness, simplicity, specificity, and you will achieve both effectiveness and style. If you are completely true to what to you is the best expression of what you want to say, your writing will be both individualistic and outstanding.

Authenticity, naturalness, makes the difference in style.

And the interesting thing about it is that it is also the easiest way to write.

Dangers from concentrating on style

There are two big dangers inherent in efforts to develop and improve style. We have referred to both before.

Subsidiary nature of style

Style is definitely and at all times a secondary quality of writing. It can never be allowed to dominate. Never forget you are writing to communicate something inside you. You are trying to pass it over to another person. That is an extremely difficult task. Style is a tool for helping you accomplish it.

In many circles, style is becoming an end in itself. *How* an action is carried out is often considered as important as *what* is done. We all know people in all walks of life who have built careers on style rather than substance or content.

Furthermore, style today has developed a further connotation. It is often given a meaning the equivalent of flair. When we say that a thing is done with style, we often mean it is done with flair. Anyone can order wine. But some people do it with style!

In this context, with emphasis on style creeping all through our society, it is no wonder writers, from eager, young, aspiring novices to old, experienced, published veterans, are fascinated by and drawn to an undue concentration on style. If you are going to write, the popular wisdom seems to dictate, you must be clever, witty, profound, sardonic, whatever. You must speak your piece with style.

And so, one would-be writer after another marches down the wide path of style without substance, proud of his cleverness, angry nobody acknowledges his art and genius, insecure enough to keep trying to "improve" his style by making it ever more striking, "farther out."

It is an obsession that haunts not only writers; it hovers over and colors many practitioners of the arts: painters, sculptors, dancers, actors.

The pursuit of style for its own sake, however, despite its prevalence, is meaningless and futile. It is an especially dangerous trap in writing. Style can enhance writing; it can make it more emphatic, clearer, more effective. But the key word is "more." Style can only increase something already there. What must be there to begin with is substance, content. If substance is missing, the best style in the world is an empty facade. Like scenery on stage, it is meaningless without the play.

The lesson can, should, and must be learned by every person trying to establish himself as an effective writer, whether in school, business, or as a professional writer. Writing, as any artistic endeavor, depends ultimately upon content, not style. That is why this book has concentrated so much on the controlling idea and its effective presentation.

Personality is secondary

The second error associated with style is similar to the first. Just as content is more important than style, so the expression of the idea through style is more important than the expression of your personality.

The fact that writing and individual writing styles do indeed also express the writer's personality is a constant source of problems in writing. Because a writer's ego is being constantly hung out for public scrutiny, there is an almost irresistible urge to dress that ego up in fancy and spectacular clothing. Every writer wants to look good. Every writer *should* want to look good.

But from that desire to look good comes the temptation to concentrate on looking good instead of concentrating on expressing the thought well.

Once part of your mind switches over to concentrating on how cleverly you can say a thing, however, you are not concentrating entirely on how clearly and effectively you can say it. That is when you will become artificial, pompous, or insincere.

Many writers, in their desire to look good, try to adopt a style that does not fit their personality. It is an effort doomed to failure, because it must be artificially maintained at all times. You must concentrate at all times on your style if you hope to maintain an artificial one. And if you do, you are not concentrating on your thought and its clear expression. At many points, you will have to choose between your style and your thought. If your style is an artificial one, your thought will suffer. Expression of personality in style, paradoxically, comes from the clear expression of what is on your mind, not the expression of what you want readers to think your personality is.

Your writing is most genuine, your style is more evident, when you are least aware that you are expressing it. You will be least aware of what style you are using when you are concentrating most on what you are saying. When you are writing most accurately and most effectively what is on your mind, your style will be at its best, and so will your writing.

So ultimately your individual style will be that which results when you are expressing yourself most clearly. Ultimately, you must work on your style as an aid to expression of your thought, not as an aid to expression of yourself. A good rule is: Never worry about what your writing says about you; instead worry about what your writing says about your controlling idea. Put in your reader's mind exactly what is in yours.

In the end, a utilitarian style is more to be prized than

a literary one. But the two are not mutually exclusive. The best literary styles are completely utilitarian. And the most utilitarian styles are highly literary.

It comes down to what we have been saying all along. Aim for simplicity, directness, and clarity. Your individual style will develop in connection with your efforts to achieve these goals. As your writing becomes clearer and more effective, you will begin to realize you do have a style, an effective style. Your boss will tell you, "Answer that complaint in your usual pleasant style." Or he will say, "Explain for the seminar next week in your clear and simple way how overhead projectors can increase sales to large corporations." Or your parents will mention how real that little incident you told them about in your last letter sounded. "We could just see you doing that." Or your editor will finally give you an assignment, instead of just sitting in judgment on your freelance efforts. "Just take your usual approach." For a writer, that is when euphoria sets in. That is when you know you have begun to express yourself clearly, directly, simply, and effectively.

That is when you know your writing has style.

Tone

Definition of tone

Style has a first cousin called tone. Tone is the real or imaginary attitude of the author toward his subject. Tone is the written equivalent of the tone of voice in which words would be spoken.

Style and tone are often confused because the word "style" is often imprecisely used when tone is meant. A writer does not usually have many different writing styles, although you hear people say he does. Usually he has a wide variety of tones that he employs to make his style more effective.

Consider the different tones used below to express the same thought, but differing attitudes of the writer toward that thought.

"New Hampshire, one of the smallest states in the Union with fewer than one million people, happens to have the first presidential primary election in the nation. Candidates use the New Hampshire primary to establish themselves as serious contenders for the nomination. The whole nation watches to see how well the candidates do in New Hampshire. As a result, the New Hampshire primary assumes an importance far beyond the number of convention delegates chosen in the primary. Presidents can be made or broken in New Hampshire." The tone is scholarly, studiously impartial, factual.

"The presidential primary election is tiny New Hampshire's third largest source of income. The residents have only a couple hundred thousand votes to sell, but they sell them dearly. Presidential candidates spend millions of dollars every four years in New Hampshire. They tramp through deep snow, surrounded by aides and security guards, seeking obscure towns and overlooked farms. New Hampshirites are thrifty and self-reliant old Yankees. They know the value of their votes. If politicians want them—and they do—they have to pay the price. They have to win an auction for them. No New Hampshirite would dream of voting for a candidate he has only met a couple of times. He wants his hand shaken till it is sore. It is the one time in four years that little New Hampshire is in the spotlight. New Hampshirites intend to keep it that way. Their law does not say New Hampshire will hold its primary during the last week of February. The law specifies New Hampshire will hold its primary at least one week before any other state in the nation does." Sardonic, lightly humorous, but mild and friendly.

"The primary is the greatest thing that happens to New Hampshire. Once every four years, the whole nation takes its lead from what presidential candidates we vote for. The rest of the country gives New Hampshire the responsibility for putting them on the right track in selecting our president. The candidates have to come up here and be judged. Our state is so small that we can all meet the candidates, talk with them, and make up our minds from first-hand knowledge. Larger states cannot hope to do this. The candidates could not reach as great a percentage of the voters personally. So we have a serious responsibility. The nation counts on our Yankee common sense to sort out the candidates for them. Once every four years, we have the opportunity to influence the course of national and international events by picking the men we think will do the best job as president." The tone is proud, supportive, cheer leader-ish.

"One tiny state, New Hampshire, is dictating the course of the nation by its undue influence on the picking of a president. One backward farm and mountain state, with people known to be unfriendly, sews up months of time from the most important people in this land, the presidential contenders, and then sits in judgment on them, even though what concerns New Hampshire is not often what the nation is concerned about. New Hampshire does not even have a city of 100,000 population. It has almost no minorities. Its major industry is tourism. How can New Hampshirites dare to exert so much influence on the course of the presidential election? How can we, concerned citizens and voters from the rest of the United States, the 'real' United States, let that happen?" Strident, hostile, angry, frustrated tone.

Tone in writing arises from the interplay of various elements. It is dictated by the frame of mind of the author toward the subject. The frame of mind of the author need not always be genuine. He may be adopting an outlook for literary or stylistic purposes. However, whatever tone the author chooses, he must maintain it through all the pertinent passages.

The writer, in trying to hit the right tone, should be aware of three elements that will influence his decision: 1. the subject, 2. the writer, and 3. the occasion.

Subject

The subject is simply what the writer is writing about. Obviously, what you are trying to say will have a big influence on the tone in which you say it.

A proposal to buy a new punch press at work will be serious, rational, dry. The subject demands it. The tone in which you describe a friend's bachelor party will be light, bantering, perhaps slightly nostalgic. The tone of a religious sermon will be dignified, scholarly, perhaps righteous.

Writer

The writer, his thinking on a subject, also affects the tone. A conservative and a liberal politician will write in completely different tones about socialized medicine. Not only will they say different things, they will say them differently, in different tones. One might be concerned and pleading, the other sarcastic and cynical. Pacifists will write in a different tone from arms manufacturers about the threat of war.

Often the writer will adopt a specific tone, place himself in a specific relationship with his readers or with his subject. Mark Twain talks through the words of Huck Finn. There is nothing wrong with this. It can be very effective. Writers should be encouraged to try different tones. You should do some experimenting with tones. Remember, we are talking tone, not style. An artificial style is an invitation to disaster. An artificial tone can be a major step towards the effective expression of your controlling idea. You are not necessarily going against your controlling idea by changing your tone. You could be augmenting it. Try being humorous when you want to be angry, sometime. You might be surprised how much more effective you can be.

Occasion

The circumstances in which you happen to be writing also have a great deal to do with the tone of a piece of writing. A valedictory, a sales pitch, a letter to a boyfriend, the recalling of a shared experience, the recitation of a harrowing adventure, each will demand a different tone.

The audience, your readers, should weigh heavily in your selection of tone. Fellow Kiwanians or Rotarians may enjoy a much lighter approach to a business accomplishment, and may understand a lot more about the background of it, than the members of the Golden Age Club or the Boy Scouts. If you are talking to friends, you will be much more informal, much lighter. The tone in which you ask your boss for a raise will be somber, hopeful, perhaps determined or pleading. The tone in which you later tell your drinking buddies how you got what you wanted from your boss will be boastful, witty, exhilarated.

With many audiences, you will have a choice of tones that you can establish. You can speak to them as equals. You can lecture them as a father. You can be their friend. You can treat them as trusted confidants. You can be an authority or a teacher.

If you are writing for employees or for teenagers, you might state matters with great definitiveness, leaving little room for doubt about your knowledge, accuracy, and ability to accomplish what you want. But if you are making a presentation to fellow doctors or to business associates, you would probably be much better off to take the tone of a colleague giving opinions.

Tone, then, is a matter of choice by the author. You can and should strive to vary tone. You should let the tone be dictated by the subject, the occasion, and your feelings as author. Again, as with all writing, you are trying to express something inside you. Human beings are not completely rational creatures. We are influenced not only by the mind but also by the heart, by feelings.

Writing should reflect that. Truly clear and effective writing is both rational and emotional. The tone is an expression of the emotion in writing. It must be controlled and it must be subservient to the effective expression of the idea. But in good writing, it is there. It is dictating the means of expression. It is aiding in the effectiveness of the writing.

CHAPTER EIGHT

Figures of Speech

Great writers generally know all the moves. They know more ways to get where they want to go than there are routes on the map. They follow each way at the appropriate time, using the phrase, the paragraph, the chapter, that will best convey their controlling idea. They score consistently because they handle the ball flawlessly. They are the Phil Fords, the Bob Cousys, the Magic Johnsons, of the written word.

In this chapter, we are going to take a look at some of those fancy moves they like to make. We have been concentrating on clear, direct, purposeful, unadorned writing because unless you can write simply, plainly and purposefully, you cannot write at all. Assuming, though, that you have made some strides toward expressing controlling ideas with maximum force, we will now touch upon the ways of elegance in writing, the ways experts decorate their work with beauty, taste and polish. Assuming we can now shoot free shots, pass the ball accurately, and dribble without always tripping, we will return again to the practice court. We want to have a go at dribbling the ball between our legs, passing behind our backs, and spotting the open man while looking the other way.

In the words of the dance, we want to leave the barre and try some leaps—basic ones to be sure, but leaps nonetheless.

Before we begin, it is necessary to insist that figures of speech have the same use in writing as everything else that goes on a page. They must make the writing more effective. They must develop and present the controlling idea. They must increase the clarity. They have no place on their own merits. If the pass behind your back and through your legs does not get the ball to the open man, it is worthless. Figures of speech must play by the same rules as any other element of writing. They must promote the controlling idea. Otherwise, they should not be used. Often, however, they do serve that function. Often a figure of speech is a stunningly simple and accurate way of making a point clearly and effectively.

Remember, this chapter is devoted to frills and fluff. Figures of speech are fun. They reflect the exhilaration of mastery rather than the plodding of the unskilled. They are decorative. Usually they are also unnecessary. You can spend your whole life writing directly and clearly, with satisfaction and pleasure, without ever developing figures of speech. But, you can also soar and dive and loop and enjoy some of the exuberance of the nightingale and Jonathan Livingston Seagull.

Simile

The first flutters above the ground for most writers are generally similes. A simile compares two unlike and unlikely objects by asserting that one is like the other. His humor was as dry as the Sahara in summer. He clung to his outmoded views as burrs clung to his pant legs. Float like a butterfly, sting like a bee. Run like a deer. From this height, the cars looked like ants.

The key to a simile is the presence of a connecting word, "like," "as," or "so." In a simile the writer announces that he is using a figure of speech. There is no deception, no chance for confusion.

Success in the use of similes depends on seeing a similarity that is not obvious. Never try to make a simile out of two objects that are really similar. It is the comparison of dissimilar objects that makes a simile work. He stood just like his twin brother. That is not a simile. It may be a good comparison, but it is not a good simile because the two objects (a man and his twin brother) are too much alike to begin with. He stood like an olive tree, bent and twisted by the winds of fate. A man is not like an olive tree, but the writer saw a similarity that shed light on the man. It is a comparison between unlike objects. It is a good simile.

There is another essential quality of a good simile. It must enlighten the reader. It must explain something about the subject of the comparison. The object must be readily understood so that it can clarify the subject. He stood like a mole in its burrow. How does a mole stand in its burrow? The simile fails because it does not touch off a responsive chord in the reader. He does not relate with the object, so he cannot use it to clarify the subject. They are as close as two coats of paint. Everyone knows how close two coats of paint are, so the simile works.

Metaphor

A metaphor is like a simile except that instead of saying a thing is like something else, a metaphor says the thing IS something else. Again, remember unlike and unlikely objects are being compared.

The girl next door is a dog. A toy store, to a child, is an enchanted forest. A presidential primary is a horse race. She was a sleek and savage jungle animal. His anger brought the curtain down on the cast party.

Beware: Many clichés are metaphors. They are still clichés and therefore unacceptable in most kinds of writing. (See page 81.) Life is just a bowl of cherries. He's sowing his wild oats. A web of intrigue held him captive.

Many times a simile can be converted into a metaphor effectively. The man was an olive tree, bent and twisted by the winds of fate. The metaphor is based on the simile used above.

A metaphor goes beyond the obvious "is" sentence, however, into all kinds of references in which the qualities of one object are attributed to another unlike object. The Mack truck playing tackle slammed into the scatback, flattening him and leaving him for dead. The trees bent toward each other in the breeze, whispering secrets and bustling with the gossip flying back and forth among them. The road clung to the side of the mountain, a discarded ribbon dropped into the trees by a bored giant. She wrapped her dignity around her, tucking in the corners to keep herself warm against the hooting and laughter of the other children.

The qualities that govern good similes also govern metaphors; namely, they must deal with basically different objects and they must enlighten the reader by pointing out a similarity with which the reader can relate.

Analogy

The third figure of speech in the simile family is the analogy. An analogy is a metaphor or simile carried through a longer passage. It is a sustained metaphor. It is usually used to help make abstract or complex thoughts clear, to make them fit into a framework with which the reader can relate.

Analogies are stock in trade for poets. They thrive on them, make profound statements through them. But analogies are not restricted to poets. The complex scientific and technological world in which we live practically demands the use of analogies for explanation. A person trying to present a complex scientific achievement to the general public almost always has to resort to analogy. There is simply too big a gap between the advances of various sciences and the knowledge of the ordinary person. Analogy is growing in importance as a tool of effective writing. It can be extremely useful for you if you are trying to explain complicated material such as the results of a study or a technological development.

Remember the example we used before of training secretaries in the use of a computer? The storage capacity was compared to a room full of filing cabinets. Each cabinet was filled with file folders. The drawers in those cabinets were assigned to specific secretaries and locks called access codes were put on them. An analogy was used to make highly technical instructions meaningful to secretaries. Writers who use such analogies in presenting technical material do a great service to their readers.

One important qualification guides such usage. Make sure the analogy works. Make sure it is not forced to the extent that it becomes muddy, or worse yet, misleading or false.

Besides length, there is another important quality that separates an analogy from a metaphor or simile. An analogy sees a number of similarities in basically different objects; a metaphor or simile sees only one. He was a grizzly bear of a man, lumbering to the stream for water. That is a metaphor. But: He was a grizzly bear of a man, lumbering on his hind legs, scratching his hairy chest, growling when annoyed, striding fearlessly through life intimidating all who came in contact with him. But his ursine qualities went beyond his gruff exterior. Basically, like a bear, he was not a predator. He preferred honey, berries and fish. He spent much time teaching his children survival as he knew it. And he was hunted, hunted by everyone who hated him, everyone who feared him, everyone who saw the chance to prove his manhood by felling the mightiest beast in the forest. Because of its complexity, that is an analogy.

Analogy, one of the most effective and satisfying figures of speech, is also one of the most frequently misused. Speech writers, commentators, advertising agencies, often use analogy to prove their point. It does not work. Analogy is a tool of description and exposition. It is never a legitimate tool of argumentation. An analogy is made between basically different objects. It can point up a similarity. But that similarity is an exception. The objects are different, except for that one similarity. Analogy cannot prove a contention by claiming that just because there is some similarity, other points of similarity must necessarily exist. This is one of the dangers in using analogies. Never, never use them to prove, only to clarify.

"Inflation is caused by higher wages for everyone. If you are watching a ball game, you could probably see better if you would stand up. If the man in front of you stands, you have to stand also, not to see better, but just to see as well. But then the people behind and around you have to stand to see. Soon everybody is standing, and nobody, including you, can see better than if all had remained seated. Wages work the same way. If you receive a raise, you have more buying power. But if everyone receives a higher wage, prices will rise to offset the higher payrolls, and nobody will be able to buy more. That is why we are applying mandatory wage-price controls. We are going to make sure the man in front of you does not stand up."

A logical analogy that clarifies and helps the reader understand inflation, right? Yes, but not a proof that higher wages cause inflation or that wage-price controls would give you more buying power. It is a valuable analogy on how inflation could sometimes be tied to higher wages. It enlightens, but it proves nothing. Used as proof that controls are needed, it demonstrates nothing more than fuzzy logic by the writer.

Allusion

Allusion is a reference to a factual, literary, or historical event without explaining it. When using allusion, the writer drops a key word into his writing and counts on that word to trigger a whole fusillade of associations in the mind of the reader. He was no Babe Ruth. McCarthy—Joe, not Gene—was his idol. His office was becoming his own private Gulag. Watergate, Shylock, Valley Forge, Mount Olympus, Casablanca, Benedict Arnold, voodoo, Hell's Angels, Garden of Eden, rattlesnake, superbowl, shark, Inquisition, Nazi, Cheshire cat, Frankenstein, Camelot, Lilliput, wizard. The word itself triggers the associations. And the associations tend to be rich, sharp, and emotional in the minds of both the reader and the writer. The very fact that the allusion is not explained or limited in any way is what makes it effective. If you try to explain an allusion or what you meant by it, you will drain it of its value. Its power comes precisely from the fact that it floats freely, taps a vein of association in the mind of the reader.

Many allusions are adjectives and therefore can be stuck into a sentence in passing, without any other support. Bunyanesque, Oedipal, radioactive, Neanderthal. They need not interrupt the flow of the thought, but they can enrich it quickly.

The normal allusion must be so well known and so easily understood that the reader does not struggle to make the associations. They must flow immediately and abundantly. There must be a basic understanding between the writer and the reader. There may be much more. The reader may have thoughts the writer did not even know; the writer may hope for some impressions that an individual reader may miss. But still there should be the central areas of agreement. Waterloo may mean many things and touch off many impressions, but it must at least bring to mind the defeat of Napoleon. Speakeasy may be a more vigorous word to older readers than to younger, but all must at least agree on the reference to night clubs during prohibition. Almost always, there must be an immediate and vivid recognition.

There are such things as obscure allusions. They play a not unimportant and at times stylish part in the history of English literature. Various schools of the past have routinely used allusions that have sent thousands of readers to reference books or have passed ununderstood. Many poets—and good ones—glory in allusions that only the literati could possibly hope to understand. Some modern poets tend almost to unintelligibility as they bury their work in allusions known only to themselves or a small "in" group. One reason poetry is not more widely read is that it is so difficult to understand. So obscure allusion does exist.

Our comment on that would be simply and bluntly: Don't *you* use it. At least, don't use it until you have moved to the literary fore and are setting the style for the rest of the writing world. Intentional obscurity is the fastest way to literary obscurity we can think of. You will have enough problems being understood; why add to them by *trying* to be unintelligible?

Allusion itself, however, readily understood allusion, is a simple and effective way to add richness and flavor to your work.

Personification

When using personification, the writer attributes to abstract ideas or inanimate objects human or animal qualities. The evening crept in on cat's paws. The eye of the movie camera watched unblinkingly every patron who entered the bank.

Terror reached out icy fingers and rubbed them slowly down her spine. Truth rode out of his heart on the same breath carrying deception from his lips. The shimmering orange heat waited to pounce on all who strayed from their tents.

Of course, terror has no fingers; heat cannot pounce. Personification can join the most abstract to the most concrete in the most unlikely manner. Because of this, it is a very poetic figure of speech. It leaves the writer great freedom of expression.

There is really only one limitation on personification and that is believability. The personification must make sense to the reader. Destruction was prancing just over the next ridge. Destruction does not prance, not even figuratively. So the personification fails. A mirage could be prancing just over the ridge, but not destruction. Destruction hovers, or rumbles, or lurks.

Personification works well with abstract material. It brings ideas to life. It is, incidentally, a form of metaphor. The two overlap regularly.

Exaggeration and understatement

Exaggeration and understatement are opposite sides of the same coin. They are two ways of intentionally warping facts for effect. Exaggeration is overstating the facts, claiming more than the truth. Understatement is expressing something with such restraint or lack of emphasis that the statement is, or seems to be, less than the whole truth.

By far the more common and better accepted of the two is exaggeration. But it is the more dangerous. It can only be used in a context where there is no danger of its being taken literally or where it makes no difference whether or not it is taken literally. Exaggeration becomes a problem, a source of slander and libel, when it is used in an unacceptable context or is taken literally. "He is suspected of having killed dozens of women." If he is only under suspicion of having killed two women, and if he is acquitted or never brought to trial in those two cases, some writer is in big trouble. "It must be 300 feet from the front door to the highway." If it is only twenty feet, the realtor is in trouble.

Aside from contexts that cry out for accuracy, however, exaggeration can generally be used, understood, and accepted. The most important key to the use of exaggeration is that the reader understand the warping of truth is intentional and not to be taken seriously. "She weighs a ton." "I swear, that fish was as long as my arm and he jerked the rod right out of my hand when he struck." "There must be fifteen million ants in our picnic basket." "I'm so hungry I could eat a horse."

While exaggeration is easy, almost natural to many writers, and readily understood by readers, its sidekick understatement is subtle, quiet, often taken for the truth by the unimaginative. It is one of the more neglected figures of speech in this age of exorbitant advertising claims and of pressure to promote, glorify, succeed. Its very rarity makes understatement highly effective and memorable when properly used. It plays nicely off the flashy exaggeration so dominant in our society. "Seattle Slew could run." "The Rockefellers generally have enough spending money." "Being president of the United States is hardly a part-time position."

Satire, irony, and parody

Satire, irony, and parody, on the surface, are forms of humor. They attain respectability as figures of speech because below the surface they are effective ways of making serious points. With them, humor is a guise covering a more deadly purpose. In fact, satire, irony, and parody often allow the writer to express thoughts that for one reason or another would be unacceptable or rejected if stated plainly.

The three are similar; but we will take each one separately and point out the differences among them as well as indicate something of their specialized usages.

Satire

Satire is a figure of speech in which derision, humor, and wit are used to point up folly and to criticize. Satire can run the full spectrum from light, guileless humor at the expense of another person, a custom, or a happening, to bitter and brutal attacks intended to destroy, change, or revolutionize. Many of today's stand-up comedians depend on satire for their success. Johnny Carson's is mostly guileless. Woody Allen and Mel Brooks put some bite into theirs. Dick Gregory and Richard Pryor are often intent on serious social commentary.

"Fill'er up, please."

"What bank do you patronize? I'll have to check your credit rating."

"I intend to pay cash."

"I'll have to have it in advance."

"It's in the armored car following me."

"OK. I'll get it from him. All right if I ask him to stick around? I don't feel safe with that much cash in the station and he might just as well take it right back to the bank for me. In fact, no sense unloading it."

Irony

Irony is a literary style employing such a contrast between apparent and intended meaning, or between what might be expected to occur and what actually has occurred, that it is plain to the reader that matters should be exactly the opposite. Irony leans on incongruities. Lyndon Johnson campaigned against Barry Goldwater in the 1964 presidential election by charging Goldwater with warmongering. He attacked Goldwater's proposals to defoliate the forests of Vietnam through which supplies went south from North Vietnam, and to bomb Haiphong Harbor. Having won the election, Johnson found he had to follow Goldwater's proposals. He defoliated the trails and he bombed Haiphong. That was ironic. What was more ironic was that these tactics did not work. Alfred Nobel, sponsor of the Nobel Peace Prize, was a munitions manufacturer. That's ironic. A few years ago, a man who claimed to be the world champion at Russian roulette was killed while practicing. That's ironic (among other things). A pilot in the Vietnam War made more than 200 bombing missions over North Vietnam. The day before he was to be sent back to the United States, he flew an extra mission in place of a sick friend and was shot down. That's ironic. We didn't have a single snowstorm in February but we had five in April. That's ironic.

The examples of irony above are intended more to give you an understanding of what irony is than to help you write irony. As far as your actual writing goes, the irony you use will be what is called verbal irony—the intentional use of a statement that is the opposite of fact. Verbal irony is a good club to have in your literary golf bag, especially if you are writing material for speeches, seminars, or instruction. "Welcome to sunny Florida," the seminar leader greets the convention members who have just stepped out of a heavy rain. "So easy even a child can assemble," says the first line of instructions for putting a bicycle together. "Ah, my cheese soufflé," says the truck driver of his scrambled eggs at the diner. "Please, I'm very sensitive," says the slob who serves him. "Computers will solve all our billing problems," quotes the accountant as the main programming disc is accidentally erased.

Parody

Parody is a literary style that ridicules by mimicry. "Let me say this about that—and I want to make myself perfectly clear—you won't have Dick Nixon to kick around anymore." When someone other than Nixon says that, it is a parody. Ironically, six years after Nixon made a similar statement, he was elected president and the kicking around began in earnest. Needless to say, that led to a lot of satire.

Satire, irony, and parody can be funny and effective. Two cautions are necessary, however.

First, do not forget that these seemingly humorous figures of speech depend on making fun of someone or something. Someone or something suffers, is mocked, is hurt by them. Be sure you want to do that. In your eagerness to be clever and to show off your wit, it is easy to forget the objects (victims) of your humor.

The second warning is that these three are difficult to use effectively. If you do not score a bull's-eye with satire, irony, and parody, you will miss completely. Humor is one of the most difficult of literary forms; and socially directed humor is a difficult form of a difficult form. If it is not absolutely accurate, and funny besides, it will backfire. You, the writer, will end up looking ridiculous if you are the least bit off the mark.

Inference

Inference refers to unstated ideas which the reader thinks of while reading. Inference deals with overtones, flavors, subtle distinctions. Every word, every sentence will make inferences as well as statements. Two hours ago, he promised he would be here soon. The money has disappeared and only two men had access to it. The president said he would sign the treaty soon and the Russian premier is coming to Washington next month. Is that lipstick on your collar? School was over three hours ago. I thought there were more cookies left. If a football player does something particularly violent, one side may claim he is hard-nosed, the other that he is dirty. The inference is completely different.

Inferences are closely allied with connotations. They both deal with meanings that are not actually stated. The distinction lies in the area of intention. An inference is always intended by the writer. A connotation may or may not be inadvertent. When a connotation is intentional, it is an inference.

Many pairs of words have essentially the same meaning but widely different inferences (or connotations): saliva and spit, creep up and sneak up, retreat and run away, brave and reckless, half empty and half full, released and fired, intelligent and smart.

Inferences are dangerous. A true inference is always intended by the writer. The problem arises when the writer uses words with inferences he did not intend, with connotations, therefore. He forgets or does not know some of the overtones. Inference is intentional. Use it as a positive force in writing. At the same time, keep one eye open in your writing for the reverse, the unwanted overtone. That is the one that will get you in trouble.

Dangers in using figures of speech

Because they are lacy frills around the edges of your controlling ideas, figures of speech are fraught with a number of dangers. Make no mistake, figures of speech can go sour. They must be carefully used or they will create more problems than they solve.

The biggest danger is that the figure of speech may miss

the mark. He ran with the awkwardness of a deer in deep water. A deer does not run in water, it swims. And a deer is associated with grace and speed. It's ironic that he expected to be elected but was not. Disappointing maybe, or surprising, but hardly ironic. Hopping into his car, he made the odyssey to his neighbor's house. That was no odyssey. Unless he went by way of Addis Ababa, the allusion is out of place.

The second danger is that figures of speech will muddy instead of clarify. Both the reference and the limitations of the figure of speech must be clear. He was a good politician, but when excited he tended to run off like water on a duck's back. The simile fails because the change in the meaning of "run off" confuses the reader. He was cool as a kumquat. A kumquat may be unknown to the reader. It is not associated with coolness. And the proximity in sound to "cucumber" irks the reader.

Finally, probably the most common error in the use of figures of speech is inconsistency. This is the error of the infamous mixed metaphor. Stick to one object of comparison. That book you thought you had lost was right under your nose; if it were a rock, it would have bitten you. When the water-skier fell, he bounced across the water like a flat stone, struggling like a wounded duck to regain his balance. The warm water embraced him, throttling his efforts to breathe. "Embrace" implies love; "throttle" implies violence. He was a grizzly of a man, lumbering to the river to drink, then scurrying back to his den. Mice, not bears, scurry.

In other words, don't switch figures of speech on short notice. Don't mix references within one figure of speech. Be consistent.

CHAPTER NINE

The Forms of Writing

A writer trying to develop a controlling idea into a written work has a limited number of literary approaches he can use to communicate effectively with the reader. These paths to effective communication are called the forms or modes of writing. They are the patterns he uses, the mechanisms for converting a controlling idea into a meaningful piece of writing.

There are four principal units that can be employed by the writer, and a number of subsidiary or minor ones. The four major approaches are narration, description, argument, and analysis. The minor ones we will consider in this chapter are dialogue, examples, and comparison and contrast. Obviously, the divisions and categories are arbitrary. Many writing experts give them different names and divide them up differently. Our purpose in offering these for your consideration is to give you the variety of writing patterns necessary to deal with whatever writing challenges you are likely to face.

Whenever you write, you are employing one or more of these methods of developing a theme. These developmental

120

modes vary greatly in their scope, their flexibility, and their suitability.

It is important to note that these methods can overlap, that more than one can be used in any piece of writing, and that more than one can be used even at the same time.

Two rules should govern your thinking as you proceed to employ these developmental forms: 1. Do not switch arbitrarily, just for the fun of it or out of carelessness. Switch with a purpose. 2. Do not lose track of which one(s) you are using.

Here, then, are the most common forms or patterns of putting controlling ideas down as written works.

Narration

Narration is the most basic form of writing. It is the one writers almost invariably tackle first, the logical first step. However, it is not only a beginning step, it is also a fundamental form used by even the most sophisticated and polished writers.

Because it serves both beginner and expert so effectively, it is an important form to master. If you can tell a story well, you will be a good writer.

What is narration? It is simply the act of describing action in the order in which it happened. It is a chronologically linear account of something. It concentrates on the action.

"Jeff peered through the bushes. He was looking for some sign of the lake. Once he found the lake, he could quickly find his way back to the picnic area. Off to the left, he heard the leaves rustle. His heart jumped. A branch snapped. Something was moving over there. Something big. It sounded to him like a truck moving through the woods. It sounded like a BEAR! Jeff froze, unable to move, unable even to scream for help. The thing moved closer. He could hear it panting.

It was in the thick bushes beside him. He could hear growls, angry sounds. The beast was making no attempt to be quiet. It was bulling recklessly through the undergrowth. Finally a scream broke from his throat. His face white, he turned to run. 'Jeff? I've been looking all over for you.' The beast stepped into view. It was his father."

Narration describes the action. It forgets everything but what is happening.

The most important characteristic of narration is that it be in order. Start at the beginning and proceed step by step to the end. Do not give the action away. Keep the reader moving through it. Don't start narration by saying, "Let me tell you about the twenty-pound pike I caught." You have ruined the story by starting at the wrong end. "Our third day in camp, we decided to explore the loggy area on the far side of the lake." That is a much better beginning. It starts at the right end and does not give anything away out of order.

Along the same line, you must make some effort in narration to ascertain exactly where the beginning of the story is. The reader is eager to get to the action. He will not be patient with an uneventful buildup. Start where the action starts, not necessarily at the temporal beginning. Get to the point. You can always put in a short explanation after you have started of how you happened to be at that point.

In the above example, evidently days one and two were uneventful, so the writer moves right to day three. If he feels the need to clarify how he happened to be in those circumstances, he can do it this way: "Our third day in camp, we decided to explore the loggy area on the far side of the lake. Harry and I had flown in for a week of fishing, but hadn't found fish the first two days." Most of the time, only a very sketchy hint of what happened before the action started will suffice. Don't start too far back. Start where the action starts.

Another key to good narration is to be specific. Don't

say he heard a noise. Instead, he heard the leaves rustle; he heard scratching behind the door; he heard a car approaching; he heard a scream in the distance; he heard stealthy footsteps, or whatever. Be specific. It is a characteristic of good writing, as we said in Chapter Four, and narration is one form of writing that depends heavily on the writer being specific.

In narration it is very easy, easier than in most other forms of writing, to lose sight of the controlling idea. It is important not to do so. Listen the next time you hear someone telling a story. Odds are he will get off the track. He will be reminded of another incident and he will take a detour. Finally he will realize he is going wrong and he will say, "But that is a whole different story; now where was I?" You've heard that many times. It ruins the spoken story, but much more it ruins the written story. In writing you are not allowed such mistakes. If you get off the track, correct it before you consider the writing finished. Take out the detour. That is the advantage of writing. You can rewrite.

In written narration you must recognize the importance of knowing what you are trying to accomplish. You will not tell everything that happened. You will tell everything that contributes to the story, that builds the controlling idea. You will eliminate everything else, no matter how interesting. That Larry got blueberry pie all over his face is funny, but it may not be important to your story about the near-drowning at the class picnic. Discipline is important in narration. The temptation is always there to say too much. Pick only the events that contribute to the controlling idea, then tell them in order and as specifically as possible.

Tone, which we discussed in Chapter Seven, is important to narration. The very rhythm of your sentences, the sound of your words will augment the action. When the pace is fast, the suspense high, go to short words and short sentences. "The bear charged. I ran." That is a much more effective way to describe the excitement and terror than the following: "My heart pounding wildly, I watched the huge, black creature from the woods begin to move towards me at a surprisingly graceful amble that quickly covered the distance. I could remain where I was no longer, so I turned and fled as quickly as my feet would cover the ground." In the second, the tone is in opposition to the action. The reader knows you would be eaten before you finished the sentence, and he can be forgiven for hoping so. When you are paddling a canoe over a still lake at dusk with the loons singing in the rushes, you may use smooth, flowing sentences and mellifluous words. But when that bear is gaining on you, the words should pound on the reader as your feet did on the ground and your heartbeat did in your temples.

Description

Description tells what an object or scene looks like. It paints a verbal picture. To succeed, the reader must see in his mind what you, the writer, saw with your eyes. Desciption is one of the toughest forms of writing. Too often, description is glossed over in favor of narration. Equally often though, description is necessary to make the narration understandable. At the very least, description is necessary to bring the narration to life.

"Jeff peered through the bushes. He knew the lake had to be in front of him, but he could not see it. To his right, the tall pines of the mature forest stood thick and silent. At their feet, a thick layer of needles hid the soil and kept it bare of new growth. He could hear a blue jay in the pines, out of sight. Ahead, where the lake should be, there was a grassy clearing, giving way after fifty feet to a copse of sumac. Behind the red sumac, the pines began again, marching up a small hill into the distance. He turned hopeful eyes to the left. Nothing. The thick underbrush extended almost to the spot where he was standing. Small maple and poplars joined with the tall marsh grass to form a shield that his eyes could not penetrate. Then he heard a branch break, directly where he was looking."

Narration is more powerful if you set the scene with description.

Many times the action is not the point of the writing. You could watch the Grand Canyon all day, be completely overawed by its grandeur, and have nothing to say about it if you depended only on narration. Nothing happened. Description is needed.

Description takes careful writing. But there are a few simple tips, some of which we have already referred to, that will go a long way towards improving your description.

First tip: Describe a thing or things in order. Don't jump from head to knees to necktie to shoes to belt. Move in a consistent, logical order in your description, the natural order in which a camera would pan across the scene or your eyes would see it. Go from right to left, or left to right, or up to down. Don't jump around.

Second tip: Be specific. State as exactly as possible what is there. You cannot describe in generalities. If you do, you will not be giving the reader enough information to paint an imaginary picture. He needs accuracy to draw from. Don't say some cows were grazing if you can say three Holsteins had escaped into the cornfield. Don't say he wore a blue suit if he was wearing a dark blue business suit, or a baby blue leisure suit with a pink flowered shirt open at the neck to show off a golden cross on a thin chain.

Third tip: Use words that appeal to the senses. The imagination operates in terms of impulses from the various senses, which impulses it calls upon to form mind pictures even when they are no longer present. Those pictures will be triggered more readily by written words that portray the textures, the sound, feel, scent, of whatever you are describing. Descriptions can bog down with the overuse of adjectives, but adjectives are often the essence of descriptions. If you are ever to use adjectives effectively, it will be for description. Don't say: "The soil was moist." Say: "The rich, black earth caked on our shoes and dampened our cuffs. In our hands, it formed into cool, moist balls instead of crumbling." Don't say: "The meadow was filled with flowers." Say: "Bees by the hundreds zoomed overhead, divebombing through the hot sun into the black eyes of the thousands of susans that turned the meadow yellow and filled the air with perfume and pollen." Give the descriptions texture. Evoke memories in the reader.

Fourth tip: Pick the significant to describe. You cannot describe everything in a scene. Zero in on the qualities that exemplify or typify what you are trying to convey, even if they are only minor parts of the scene. The man may be dressed in perfectly ordinary clothes; it is the scar on his left cheek that makes him look sinister and gives the texture of his personality. The bulge under his arm may be hard to see, but it indicates the presence of a gun and is worth describing. The little lever on the side of the huge punch press would pass unnoticed during most inspections, but it sets the machine on repeat, an important feature in your sales pitch. Also, if the description is interlocked with a narration, be sure to describe all the elements that are later important to the narrative. That big tree may be insignificant in a description of the farmyard, but if the escaped killer is later going to hide behind it, the reader has to know it is there.

Fifth tip: Establish and maintain your focal point. Remember in description you are providing eyes for the reader. Eyes see things from a specific point. Don't suddenly describe the back of something. Be consistent. You may have to describe the back also, but only after your narration has walked the reader around. You can confuse the reader as easily by changing your viewpoint as you can by jumping from one part of the scene to another in no apparent order.

The house looked abandoned. The black asphalt roofing was still sound, but the gray paint below had peeled and blotched. The upper windows were shuttered and boarded over with plywood. The front door was tightly shut, but the shutter on the window to the left of the door had worked loose and was creaking gently in the breeze. Nancy crossed the clearing swiftly, in a semicrouch. She threw herself to the ground below the window. Carefully, inch by inch, she raised her head until she could see through the window. NOW you can describe the inside of the house.

Argumentation

Argumentation is writing that proves the truth of an assertion.

Argument appeals directly to the intellect, to reason and logic. It is not at all concerned with the emotions, except insofar as emotional appeals can sway judgments and decisions. It establishes and maintains the controlling idea by cold facts, by inescapable conclusions.

Argument can be used by itself throughout a piece of writing. It is a self-sufficient way of developing a controlling idea. Often a strictly logical argument is the most effective way of proceeding, as when trying to sell an idea at the office. Frills are often unneeded in such circumstances. Leave them out; cut the writing down to its bare logical bones.

On the other hand, pure argumentation tends to be unexciting. It tends to be dry and of limited interest. Many times you can be writing in circumstances where unexciting, dry, factual writing is important, even necessary. Many times frills are just that. If such is the case, by all means stick to strict argumentation.

More often argument benefits in its appeal and readability from being mixed with some of the more appealing, less businesslike ways of developing a piece of writing. Argument that is disguised in narration or dialogue, for instance, can hold the reader more effectively than plain argumentation. Argument broken up by examples or comparisons is often more effective than argument standing alone. If the circumstances allow it, or if you wish to lighten the circumstances or make them less formal, one good way to improve argumentation is by peppering your arguments with spicier methods of writing.

Strict argumentation: Even in inflationary times a house is a good investment for a young couple because traditionally housing prices have risen faster than inflation. With an expanding population, demand for housing will continue to increase. Owning a house becomes a form of saving because couples are building equity. And a house gives satisfaction to the couple living in it.

Argumentation augmented with narration and dialogue: It cost Jim and Janet every penny of their savings, but they managed to buy a two-bedroom ranch house on Maple St. Jim's brother was appalled. "Put it in savings. When the housing market collapses, you won't lose it all."

But Jim was adamant. "Housing has continued to appreciate in both inflationary and recessionary times. It is a better investment than savings."

"So far. But the bottom is due to fall out."

"The population is increasing faster than houses can be built. As long as that is the case, demand should be strong."

Jim's brother looked at Janet. She was pregnant again. They already had a two-year-old, he mused. What if something happened and they had large medical expenses? He tried again. "With savings, if an emergency arises, the funds are available. What do you do if little Jimmy gets sick?"

"Our company has good coverage for employees' families."

Jim obviously had thought out all the arguments. His smug attitude was irritating his brother. "But the money is not available to you for any other purposes."

"Yes it is," Jim replied. "We have already used it in the most enjoyable way we know. This house gives us more pleasure than any other use we could make of the money. We love it here."

Argument spiced with examples: When inflation hit double figures, car prices rose 12 percent. Clothing went up 7 percent. Food went up 11 percent. All are disposable goods with little or no resale value. Housing prices rose 27 percent during the same period. And houses can be resold for that value. One reason for that is that after World War II there was a tremendous increase in population. These post-war babies now have the income to purchase houses. Jim and Janet are post-war babies. Now married five years, they recently invested all their savings in a small house. They love it. The pleasure owning their own home gives them makes it money well spent. At the same time, their monthly house payments build equity for them. They are actually increasing their savings as they enjoy their house.

There is, though, a danger buried in presenting argumentation mixed with other forms of writing. The danger is that you will sacrifice order or clarity. The reader must know what you are doing, understand the arguments being presented, even though they are presented as narration or example. If you sprinkle lighter forms of writing into argumentation, be sure you keep your eye on the controlling idea. Be sure not only the arguments but also the interludes do indeed contribute to the presentation of proof for your controlling idea. They must be to the point, not by the by.

Analysis

Analysis is the examination of the elements that make up a controlling idea. It is the dissecting of the controlling idea into parts so the reader can come to understand and appreciate both the parts and the whole. When he understands all the parts more clearly, he will presumably understand the controlling idea more clearly and effectively.

Analysis is especially effective when dealing with obscure, complicated, or comprehensive ideas. Remember, you have reached the controlling idea through a mental process involving many steps. The writing may have to break that idea back into its components before the reader can appreciate the controlling idea. This breaking down of a controlling idea into components is known as analysis.

"Not even the president can control the federal budget because (1) much of the money is allocated in previous years and already committed, (2) federal programs interact and one demands another, so that it is impossible to cut back in individual areas, (3) social welfare programs have become a right rather than a gift for many citizens, and (4) Congress can command the spending of money by the president."

Analysis in its pure form tends to suffer from the same weaknesses as argumentation; namely, it is dry and uninteresting. The problem can be solved by joining analysis with other forms of writing. When doing so, again, it is important to keep the writing clear and to keep the material relevant and pertinent to the controlling idea.

Dialogue

Besides the four major forms of writing we have been discussing, there are numerous less common ones. Dialogue is the first of these we will consider.

Dialogue is using words in the mouths of real or imagined characters to advance the controlling idea.

"Jerry, if you bring that chicken in here, I'm leaving."
"But where am I going to keep him? He can't stay out in the snow."

"Young man, you should have thought about that before you bought him."

"I didn't buy him. I traded my parka for him."

"You what?"

Dialogue is an effective tool in writing. Its use is often overlooked in serious, functional writing. It should not be. Smart, professional communicators use dialogue to accomplish results they cannot attain in other ways. The advantages of dialogue are many. Check any magazine or brochure. Notice the effective use of dialogue to stimulate your interest in the advertisements.

Dialogue tends to hold the reader's interest and attention better than simple exposition. Another advantage is the flavor that can be brought into writing through dialogue. The spoken word is often completely different from the written, in its color, implications, and character. Dialogue can capture that flavor in writing. A third effective use of dialogue is in the expression of conflicting opinions. Different characters can express diverse and contradictory points of view.

Examples

Examples rank among the minor forms of writing. They are usually incomplete ways of expressing a controlling idea. They almost never stand by themselves. Almost always they have to be supported by other forms of writing and they have to be set in context. They merely express a controlling idea in specific events.

Still, examples are an important way of developing your thoughts because they are so specific. Remember, the more specific the writing, the more understandable it is likely to be. A good example can do more for a clear understanding of what you are trying to say than reams and reams of general writing.

Care must be taken with examples, however. The three basic rules governing the use of examples are: An example must be clear; it must prove what you want it to prove; and it must be capable of easy interpretation by the reader.

"The old sometimes remember events of forty or fifty years ago, but cannot remember what happened an hour or a day ago. For instance, my grandmother can cite chapter and verse about my mother's childhood during the Great Depression. My mother, it seems, landed a job in a textile mill and earned enough money to hold the family together, even though she was still in her teens. 'Tired she used to come home,' my grandmother still recalls. 'My heart would bleed for her so young and tired, with her dress wrinkled and her face smudged. I can see her now, walking into the kitchen and handing her father her paycheck. Proud she was, but still only a little girl.' But ask my grandmother what she had for breakfast or whether she has been to the grocery store today, and she will give you a blank stare."

The example is clear, easy to interpret, and proves the point about the memory of the aged. Here are some variations on the same paragraph:

"The old sometimes remember events of forty or fifty years ago, but cannot remember what happened to them an hour or a day ago. For instance, my grandmother was alive during the Great Depression; but she often does not remember whether or not she has gone to the grocery store." The example is not clear. It thus fails to advance the controlling idea.

"The old sometimes remember events of forty or fifty years ago, but cannot remember what happened to them an hour or a day ago. For instance, my grandmother turns down her hearing aid. Since she cannot hear what is being said, she often brings up something that has just been discussed."

The example does not prove the controlling idea. It proves something else entirely. It is a bad example.

"The old sometimes remember events of forty or fifty years ago, but cannot remember what happened to them an hour or a day ago. For instance, my grandmother remembers every opera she ever attended but cannot remember any baseball games." The example is not easily interpreted. For it to be acceptable as an example, the reader must be told she has not gone to an opera in thirty-five years but she now goes to see the Yankees eighty times a season.

Examples have to be used with care and with attention to the traps that render them ineffective. But if they are used properly, they are among the most effective forms of writing available. They are clear, specific, to the point, and effective— the very qualities we are trying to develop.

Comparison and contrast

Comparison and contrast are ways of developing writing by pointing up similarities or differences between two objects. Comparisons are usually between like things—two cities, two books, two persons, etc. Metaphors, similes, and analogies differ from normal comparisons in that they deal with unlike objects. Comparisons are normally made between similar things.

Contrast is the opposite of comparison. Contrast clarifies by pointing up differences rather than similarities. He was no Einstein. We seemed 100 miles from the nearest human being, at peace with nature, until the teenagers in the next van began playing rock music. The difference between him and a skunk is that a skunk can at least defend itself.

Contrast bears all the characteristics of comparison. The chief danger in using comparison and contrast is the same one we dealt with under analogy. All three are tools of clarification, never of proof. They explain an idea, make it more comprehensible. They never establish its truth. It is a simple fact of logic that cannot be violated without damaging credibility and effectiveness. Never prove something by comparison or contrast. Do use comparison and contrast to make clear. They do that effectively.

CHAPTER TEN

The Mechanics

There are infinite nuances to human thought. To express such variety, the language also has to be complex. The English language possesses the required complexity and subtlety. It is an excellent tool for communication, capable of high degrees of sublimity and intricacy.

The writer, searching for every edge he can find to communicate effectively, must, *must*, MUST use the language accurately. He must follow all those generally agreed-upon conventions that make up English. Clarity depends on it. So does effectiveness. The writer who is trying to communicate effectively is defeating himself if he uses language in any but the agreed-upon way.

There is another, much less important reason for using language correctly. To do so is impressive. When you are communicating with someone, you are making a statement not only about your subject but also about yourself. If you are using the language correctly (or incorrectly), your readers will notice. They will make a judgment about you based upon your command of the language. Put in its bluntest form, you will score higher grades, get your way more often, increase your chances of being published, and be more likely to prosper in business if you represent yourself well in writing.

Because of the importance of proper use of language as a tool of effective communication, we are going to deal in this chapter with some of the most common misuses of language, some of the most common errors, the most common violations of the commonly agreed-upon conventions for communicating in English.

The structure of language breaks down into four parts: diction, spelling, grammar, and punctuation. Giving words their proper meaning is called diction. Spelling is the agreed-upon arrangement of letters to symbolize words. Grammar is the arrangement of words in meaningful patterns which show the relationships of the words to one another. Punctuation is the accepted designation of marks to clarify and explain the relations in sequences of words.

To make a piece of writing communicate effectively, you must use to the fullest, and properly, the mechanics that make up the language.

The goal of this chapter is to point out some of the most common errors in diction, spelling, grammar, and punctuation. The material in this chapter is not intended to be inclusive. Almost every expert has his own list of pet peeves, errors that offend him. Here we are listing some we consider common.

This material is for learning, not research. If you are not sure of the meaning or usage, look in the dictionary or in a grammar book, not here. The material here is not intended to be definitive. On the other hand, if you can avoid making the mistakes in the use of the language described here, if you make it a point to use these basic rules and examples correctly, you will probably eliminate most of the errors in English usage you are now making. Therefore, don't just read through the material in this chapter; memorize it.

Twenty-five misused pairs of words

1. Adverse and averse. Adverse means against, hostile. Averse means reluctant. "I am not averse to going, except in adverse weather."

2. Affect and effect. Use "affect" as a verb and "effect" as a noun. Affect means influence; effect means outcome or result. "He affected the course of action, but had no effect on the outcome." (Each has one rare exception. Effect can be a verb when it means "totally bring about" as in: "He effected an escape." Affect has special usage as a noun meaning roughly an emotion, especially in psychiatry. If you forget both exceptions and always make affect a verb and effect a noun, you will be right 99 times out of 100.)

3. Allusion and illusion. Allusion means reference; illusion means false mental image. "He was under the illusion that a mere allusion to his name would cause all to bow." Also look out for delusion, a false belief. "The optical illusion did not change his delusion about the desert."

4. Cite, sight and site. Cite means quote. Sight means view or scene. Site means location. "He cited the building on the site as one of the most interesting sights in the city."

5. Compliment and complement. Compliment is an expression of admiration or praise. Complement means something that completes or augments. "He paid me a compliment when he said my scarf was a nice complement to my complexion." Both can also be verbs.

6. Continual and continuous. Continual means repeated again and again. Continuous means without interruption. "The continual interruptions and the continuous noise gave me a headache."

7. Contemptible and contemptuous. Contemptible refers to an object; contemptuous refers to a subject or person. "I

am contemptuous of your contemptible habit of smoking."

8. Council, counsel and consul. Council is an advisory body. Counsel is the advice given. Consul is a government official. "The American consul in Florence was able to give better counsel to travelers than the city council." Of the three, only counsel can be a verb.

9. Demure and demur. Demure means reserved in manner. Demur means to object or decline. "She was too demure to demur, even though she did not want the job."

10. Discrete and discreet. Discrete means distinct, separate. Discreet means unobtrusive or respectful. "A discreet person knows that a solution can consist of discrete parts."

11. Disinterested and uninterested. Disinterested means unbiased. Uninterested means not interested. "As a disinterested spectator, I would say he is uninterested in the game."

12. Elicit and illicit. Elicit means to bring forth, draw out. Illicit means illegal, not allowed. "We elicited from him that their marriage was illicit."

13. Emigrant and immigrant. An emigrant moves out of a country. An immigrant moves into one. "Emigrants from Europe were the principal immigrants to the United States."

14. Evoke and invoke. Evoke means to call forth, inspire. Invoke means to call upon, appeal to. "When he invoked the name of Roosevelt, he evoked a response from the Democrats."

15. Exalt and exult. Exalt means to raise up, praise. Exult means to rejoice. "She exulted when her husband was exalted to the highest position in his lodge."

16. Excessively and exceedingly. Excessively means inordinately. Exceedingly means to an unusual degree. "We clapped excessively because we were exceedingly proud."

17. Imply and infer. Imply means to indicate without

saying. Infer means to understand something that was not actually said. Speakers and writers imply. Listeners and readers infer. "I infer from what was said that they were implying a crime had been committed."

18. Ingenious and ingenuous. Ingenious means clever or imaginative. Ingenuous means simple or innocent. "It was an ingenious solution to come from such an ingenuous little girl."

19. Loath and loathe. Loath means hesitant or reluctant. Loathe means to hate. "He was repulsive, but being a Christian I was loath to loathe him."

20. Marital and martial. Marital concerns marriage. Martial concerns war. Purists insist there is a difference. "His marital problems resulted from his study of the martial arts. He broke her neck demonstrating a karate chop."

21. Moral and morale. Moral means ethical, upright. Morale is a state of mind. "The minister was such a moral man that his morale tended to be high."

22. Persecuted and prosecuted. Persecute means to harrass. Prosecute means to take to court. "They prosecuted him for tax evasion, but many thought they were just persecuting him."

23. Principal and principle. Principal means main or chief. Principle means standard or tenet. "The principal reason Thomas More was executed was that he would not compromise his principles."

24. Sensual and sensuous. Sensuous refers to pleasure and has positive connotations. Sensual refers to pleasure and has negative connotations. The distinction is slight, but important. "She took a relaxing, sensuous bath before going to a sensual strip show."

25. Troop and troupe. Soldiers and boy scouts come in troops; actors and singers come in troupes. "A troupe of acrobats entertained the troops at the front."

Grammar errors

Sentence fragments

A sentence fragment is a group of words punctuated as if it were a sentence. In fact it is not a complete sentence. A complete sentence must consist of at least a subject and a verb. It must stand alone in meaning as a complete unit; it must not be dependent upon another subject or verb in order to be complete. A sentence fragment does not stand alone. If it has a subject and verb, they are in subsidiary clauses rather than making up the main clause.

We decided to cross the street. Although the traffic was heavy and there were six lanes in each direction. Not to mention the ice. Or the group of kids who were waiting patiently on the far curb for the light to change so they could cross to our side. The flow of traffic stopping in both directions as the light switched to red. Before we could reach the far curb.

In the above passage, only the first short sentence is a complete sentence. It has a principal subject and verb. The rest are sentence fragments.

The most common kind of sentence fragment is the subordinate clause written as though it were a self-sufficient statement. In the following examples, the first statement is a sentence; the second is a sentence fragment consisting of a subordinate clause.

Novice runners frequently sustain injuries to the feet and legs. Because they do not wear properly designed shoes.

Many traffic accidents could be avoided. If drivers were more cautious.

140

Young children are surprisingly agreeable companions. Except when they are tired, hungry, or ill.

Sentence fragments can be corrected in two easy ways. The fragment can be converted into a self-sufficient sentence by adding a principal subject and verb, or by converting the subject and verb into principal ones; or the fragment can be combined with the preceding sentence to form one sentence.

Here are some examples of fragments from above that are converted into sentences by changing the verbs and subjects into principal ones, or by adding necessary verbs and subjects.

We decided to cross the street. The traffic was heavy, as there were six lanes in each direction. The street was covered with ice. Some kids were waiting patiently on the far curb for the light to change so they could cross to our side. The flow of traffic stopped in both directions as the light switched to red. We were unable to reach the far curb, however, before it switched back to green.

The following sentences, also taken from above, are sentences formed by joining fragments with preceding sentences.

Because they do not wear properly designed running shoes, novice runners frequently sustain injuries to their feet and legs.

Many traffic accidents could be avoided if drivers were more cautious.

Except when they are tired, hungry, or ill, young children are surprisingly agreeable companions.

This solution, joining the fragment to the sentence, works well for most types of fragments, not only those consisting of subordinate clauses.

He was the ideal tour guide. Knowledgeable, affable, unflappable. Make it one sentence: He was the ideal tour guide—knowledgeable, affable, unflappable.

Adroitly balancing the demands of her profession, her marriage, her three children, and her civic responsibilities. Dr. Mary Smith wrote an article for the local weekly newspaper. Change it to: Dr. Mary Smith wrote an article for the local weekly newspaper explaining how she adroitly balances the demands of her profession, her marriage, her three children, and her civic responsibilities.

Sentence fragments are incorrect grammar. Experienced writers, however, occasionally use sentence fragments for stylistic effect. Fragments, like short sentences, can quicken the pace of writing. They can also give it the flavor of speech, and are thus sometimes appropriate to informal prose.

The doorknob turned. Slowly. She stared at it transfixed. The chain! Was it on? Yes. The door moved. Opening cautiously inward. Toward her. As far as the chain would allow. Crash! The chain shattered. The door burst off its hinges. Falling end over end down the stairs. Smashing the table below. Resting on the floor at her feet. She looked up. A man in a black ski mask stood in the doorway. Gigantic. Muscular. Looking down at her. MOVING down at her.

The fragments come in short breaths that reflect her terror.

Luke slouched against the wall, his pipe hanging from the corner of his mouth. "Saw Nelson the other day. Looking old. Hair gone. Hard to recognize. That episode up in the canyon. He's never been the same since. Drifting off all the time. Talks of the past. The log drive of '35. Stepping into the jam. Finding the key log. Prying it free. Losing his leg. Almost drowning. Better pull himself together. Hard to remember. One time, he was the best there was."

Sentence fragments can be effective tools. More often, especially for the inexperienced, they are simply errors in grammar. Even if intentional, they will look like errors unless carefully and cleverly used. Why risk it? Postpone experimenting with the deliberate use of sentence fragments until your control of sentence structure is consistent and routine. Like artists, writers should violate the rules of their craft only after mastering them.

Agreement of subject and verb

Most people understand the laws governing subject/verb agreement. They know that a singular subject requires a singular verb and a plural subject requires a plural verb. They are not confused by a pair of subjects; they automatically use a plural verb with two subjects joined by "and" and a singular verb with two subjects joined by "or." When faced with two subjects, one singular and one plural, joined by "or," they may hesitate briefly, but they usually come up with the rule that the verb agrees with the closer subject. "Either a rabbit or squirrels have been eating the seedlings in our garden."

As long as the sentence is short and the subject clearly identifiable, few problems arise. It is when sentences become long and complicated, or when the subject and verb are separated by interrupting material, that writers run into trouble. The coach, as well as the players and trainers, object to locker-room interviews. "Coach" is the subject. It is singular, so the verb should be "objects," singular. A large building—maybe a distillery—in the background is undergoing renovations; and this, along with the people's fine clothing and radiant smiles, suggest a healthy economy. The subject of the sentence is "this," which is singular. The verb should be "suggests."

(Notice in the last example that the sentence itself is unwieldy. The writer tried to join the observation about the renovation of a building with the prosperous populace. To do so, he used the word "this" to refer to a whole clause instead of a specific word. It is no wonder he lost sight of the subject. Moral: Keep your sentences simple and you will avoid many subject/verb agreement problems.)

Pronouns provide a special set of subject/verb agreement problems. Specifically, the singular pronoun is often joined to a plural verb, as in "It don't make any difference," or, "He don't need any help." The singular form of the verb is "doesn't." It must always be used with singular subjects.

One more category is worth mentioning under agreement of subject and verb: nobody, one, each, somebody, everyone, and the like. They are normally singular and take singular verbs. Thus the following sentences are all correct: "In the army, nobody volunteers or he will be given extra assignments." "One of the valves that control the water flow is stuck." "Football players can play basketball; but if one does he will have to make some adjustments." "Each of the students going to the party has to complete his homework first."

Dangling and misplaced modifiers

The term "dangling modifier" is used to describe a phrase, usually a verb phrase or a clause, that the writer has failed to anchor to any specific word in a sentence. "Attired in a warm parka, waterproof pants, and a wooly red hat with a blue and red tassel, the mountain did not look as formidable." Of course, the mountain did not dress that way at all. The reader will chuckle and then wonder about you and your writing.

To avoid giving your readers cause for merriment at the expense of your credibility, be especially careful of phrases and clauses that introduce a sentence. Most dangling modifiers occur at the beginning. Make sure word groups at the beginning are not cast adrift; anchor them firmly to the rest of the sentence by joining them directly to a specific word, the one they modify. Usually the key word has been omitted. Put it back in. "If taken in large quantities like a whole six-pack, a person can become obnoxious." It is beer, not a person, that has to be taken in large quantities. Say so. "If taken in large quantities like a six-pack, beer can make a person obnoxious." "After lifting and carrying for three hours, the warehouse was put back neatly in order." Anchor the modifier thus: "After lifting and carrying for three hours, we had put the warehouse neatly back in order."

Misplaced modifiers are close cousins of dangling modifiers. A misplaced modifier is a word, phrase, or clause, that seems to modify one word in the sentence when in actuality it refers to another. The ambiguity can be resolved by putting the modifier next to the word it modifies.

"After flying for 200 miles, the sailor saw the seagull alight on the mast of his ship." "Alone in his den all winter, berries and fish could not sate the bear's appetite." "Tom had a hard time visualizing the hot sun plowing through snow up to his hips." The modifier is separated from the word it modifies in all the above sentences. They should read: "The sailor saw the seagull, after flying for 200 miles, alight on the mast of his ship." "Alone in his den all winter, the bear could not sate his appetite on berries and fish." "Plowing through snow up to his hips, Tom found it hard to visualize the hot sun."

Pronouns

Pronouns are good allies of a writer because they make it easy to eliminate undesirable repetition. But pronouns, like many allies, can be troublesome at times. The problem with pronouns is that they are the only words left in the English language that change their form according to their function in the sentence. A pronoun used as an object often has a different form from a pronoun used as a subject. Thus: *I* saw it; but it also saw *me. She* looked at *her. He* jumped; but I tried to stop *him.*

The rule is simple. There is a form of the pronoun for each usage. You must use whichever form is required by the sentence. Probably no aspect of the English language causes more errors in common speech than misuse of pronouns. The biggest offender seems to be the pronoun "I." In the Midwest, the objective form (me) is often used as the subject. "John and me went to town." In the Northeast, the subjective form (I) is often used as an object. "Between you and I, money is no problem." "He" and "she" also manage to be misused in the same way. "You and him make a good couple." It should be: "You and he make a good couple."

An especially confusing case is presented by the relative pronoun "who." The objective case, both singular and plural, is "whom." Thus: "I can't see the man whom you pointed out," and "There are seven workers whom management refuses to promote."

Remembering to use "whom" when the relative pronoun is the object of a verb or preposition is complicated enough, especially because often the verb, of which it is the object, comes behind it in the sentence.

But English experts have managed to complicate it further. It is generally agreed today that it has become acceptable to use "who" after a verb in informal speech or writing. This is a case where the language, a living language in constant use, is changing. In other words, so many people misuse "who" so often as an object the experts have given up trying to keep people using the more proper "whom." They are allowing "who" unless the formal context demands accuracy.

The problem is: what is a formal or informal situation? The guidelines are nebulous. Obviously, a legal document is formal and a letter to a friend is informal. But there is a large gray area of borderline formality, such as student papers, memos to your superiors, and talks at service clubs.

Our advice is to be conservative. You are never wrong using "whom" as the object of a verb or preposition. You are sometimes wrong using "who." So if you have any doubt, use "whom."

Part of the problem in making pronouns agree is of recent origin. It has followed from feminine awareness. The English language uses the masculine form for impersonal discourse. Thus: "A person who wants to succeed must define his goals." The use of the masculine gender (*his* goals) is sexism in language. The masculine has always been used in English. In the last few years, feminists have objected. Linguists aware of the sexism have tried to find alternate solutions. Nonlinguists aware of the sexism have begun using the plural form of the pronoun in such cases because there is no distinction in form of the plural pronoun. Thus: "Anyone who continually has headaches should see *their* doctor."

In all such impersonal cases, the traditional word is the masculine "him." But more and more experts are coming to accept the use of both masculine and feminine singulars in such cases. "A person who wants to succeed must define his or her goals (or his/her goals)." "Anyone who continually has headaches should see his or her doctor." There is also presumably nothing wrong with the more militantly feminist preference for intentionally picking the feminine in impersonal discourse. Thus: "If somebody is qualified for a job you have open and *she* applies for it, give it to *her*." On this point, the language is in a state of flux.

One point is clear, however. Only the singular is acceptable. The plural is wrong. It is the gender of the pronoun that is in question, not the number.

Verb tenses

The tense (past, present, future) of a verb is another problem area in grammar.

Tense is used to indicate the time at which an event is taking place. It can be measured against the time at which the writing occurs (Last night I noticed some of our typewriters were missing. I am checking them today. If I find some have disappeared, I will call the police tomorrow."), or it can be measured against the time of other action in the writing ("John had noticed some typewriters missing. He checked the next day, found seven unaccounted for, and decided to call the police.").

Consistency is the key to proper use of tenses. Tense establishes a point of view similar to that in description. The chosen tense must be maintained not only inside a sentence but often also between sentences or between paragraphs. "He went to the store; he stopped for a drink, talked with some friends, and came home late for dinner." "I will go to the store; I will stop for a drink; and I may be late for dinner." Be consistent.

In business writing, theses, letters, lectures, and speeches, the tense is usually dictated by the time the writer is writing or going to speak. In narration, the tense is usually related to other action in the writing, rather than tied to outside events. Narration is commonly put in the past tense, although the narrative present can also be used effectively, especially to convey immediacy and excitement.

The tense of all verbs in narration is tied to the narrative tense being used. The relation of the verb to the narrative, not to the time of the writing, becomes important. "He heard the sound and turned. Had he remembered to lock the door? He knew he would soon regret that oversight." All the verb tenses are dependent upon the narrative past being used. "He hears a sound and turns. Has he remembered to lock the

148

door? He knows he will soon regret that oversight." In the second example, all the tenses are dependent upon the narrative present.

If the narrative past is the basic tense being used, an event that is in the past in relation to the events being narrated should be put in a form that indicates a double past. That form is called the past perfect. It is usually indicated by the helping word "had." "He heard the door open. He had not locked it." "Had not locked" indicates the event happened further in the past than the narrative past being used.

Passive voice

The English language is a powerful tool for describing action. English words, especially verbs, carry great vitality and convey movement and life. Perverse writers, though, have found a method of sapping those vital English verbs of their strength. That way is the use of the passive voice. Bureaucrats and researchers are consistent offenders in this regard. They use the passive voice, presumably, because it is a safer, more cautious way of writing. The passive voice can be hedged more easily. It is impersonal and seems less definite.

What is the passive voice? It is a method of speaking that converts objects into subjects and then has the verb act upon the subject rather than the usual object. "Captives were taken by the guerrillas." "The rats were injected with 500ccs of toxin a day." "The occupant shall not be evicted, even if the rent is unpaid."

The opposite of the passive voice is the active voice. It is the normal and vital way of expressing thoughts. If action is involved, the active voice is almost always more effective. It bristles with life. The passive voice just sits there and lets things happen to it. The above examples, converted to the active voice, would be much livelier. "The guerrillas took many captives." "The scientists injected 500ccs of toxin a day into the rats." "If an occupant does not pay his rent, the landlord still cannot evict him."

Sometimes the passive voice is necessary. Sometimes you can't get around it. Reserve it for those occasions only. Don't rob your sentences of their vitality by putting them in the passive voice. The active is much more effective.

Punctuation problems

Commas

Do not join sentences with a comma. Use a period between sentences; or, if the thoughts expressed in the two sentences are closely related, use a semicolon. The error of using a comma between sentences is called a comma splice. Professional writers occasionally use comma splices for the same reason they sometimes use sentence fragments—for stylistic effect. Our advice is the same as it was for sentence fragments. Do not experiment with comma splices until you have mastered the fundamentals of sentence structure.

Do not write:

"Portsmouth, New Hampshire, is situated at the mouth of the Piscataqua River, in the eighteenth century it was an important seaport."

"The accident occurred at the corner of Chestnut and Main, the victim was rushed to the nearby hospital."

"Modern typewriters correct mistakes automatically, with automatic corrections secretaries should have more time."

Instead write:

"Portsmouth, New Hampshire, is situated at the mouth of the Piscataqua River. In the eighteenth century, it was an important seaport."

"The accident occurred at the corner of Chestnut and Main. The victim was rushed to the nearby hospital."

"Modern typewriters correct mistakes automatically; with automatic corrections, secretaries should have more time."

The use of a period or a semicolon gives equal weight to both ideas. If you wish to give more weight to one or the other idea, you have some other options for correcting the comma splice. You can, for instance, convert one sentence into a phrase or clause. "Situated at the mouth of the Piscataqua River, Portsmouth, New Hampshire, was once an important seaport." The above sentence stresses the historical information. Conversely, if you wish to stress the geographical location, you can write: "Portsmouth, New Hampshire, which was once an important seaport, is situated at the mouth of the Piscataqua River." If you wish to show a cause and effect relationship between the two ideas, you should write: "Its location at the mouth of the Piscataqua River made Portsmouth, New Hampshire, an important seaport."

A comma splice can be corrected in any number of ways. If you at least replace the offending comma with a period or a semicolon, you will improve the clarity and correctness of your writing.

An exception: Short sentences (main clauses) can be joined by commas if they are written in series: "I laughed, I cried, I screamed in terror."

You should use a comma before "and," "or," "but," "nor," "for" when these conjunctions are used to join independent clauses. An independent clause is part of a sentence but has a verb and makes a complete statement. "Jonathan visited Rome and Paris last summer, but he did not see the Colosseum or the Louvre." The difference between this rule and the rule governing comma splices is that here the independent clause is an integral part of the thought, while in comma splices the two thoughts are separate. Notice that a comma is placed before the conjunction "but" because it joins two clauses. No comma is placed before "and," nor is one placed before "or" in this sentence. "And" and "or" connect direct objects, not clauses in this particular example. "And" and "or" obviously would take commas if they were joining independent clauses.

The comma between independent clauses is occasionally omitted if the clauses are short. "We yelled but we heard no answer." "He came and he went." "The car is an antique or it is junk."

Use a comma after a long introductory phrase or clause. "Not wanting to inconvenience his aunt or uncle, he reserved a room at a local hotel." "Although I do not usually enjoy reading murder mysteries, I stayed up past midnight reading *Murder on the Calais Coach.*"

Use a comma to set off parenthetical or nonessential material. "Jack Jones, the head linesman, placed the ball on the ten-yard line." "Nutrition is, in my opinion, an underrated science."

Notice that in the last two examples, the information between the commas is not essential to the meaning of the sentences. A clause that contains such nonessential material is called a "nonrestrictive clause" and is set off by commas. A clause that contains information that cannot be dispensed with is called a "restrictive clause." A restrictive clause is *not* set off by commas. "The woman who just arrived is the senator's daughter." "What have you done with the book that I bought yesterday?" The clauses in these examples supply the information necessary for the reader to identify the woman or the book in question.

Use a comma to prevent misreading. Whenever there is a possibility that the reader may stumble over a word group, use a comma to keep him moving through the sentence smoothly. "Underneath the ship was covered with barnacles." Without the comma, "Underneath the ship" seems to go together as a prepositional phrase. It should be: "Underneath, the ship was covered with barnacles." "While the wind was still strong men came out to put up the tent." It should be: "While the wind was still, strong men came out to put up the tent."

Semicolons and dashes

The semicolon and the dash give the writer two key allies in the war against sentence monotony. The semicolon and the dash can help a writer vary the pace of sentences, change their rhythm, and give them momentum. They often should be used where the first inclination is to use a comma plus a conjunction (instead of a semicolon) or parentheses (instead of a dash). Whereas semicolons are lean, commas plus conjunctions are flabby. Dashes are quick and conversational while parentheses are academic and ponderous.

Use a semicolon to join main clauses when the ideas being expressed are closely related. "Hyperactivity in children has been linked to food additives; when placed on an additive-free diet, many hyperactive children return to normal." "Bermuda is a popular tourist destination; last year half a million tourists visited the island." "One of the candidates supports the tax increase; the others oppose it."

Notice that in these cases, the sentences could be joined

in other ways. Comma/conjunction could be used; separate sentences could be used. The semicolon tends to make the sentences livelier, quicker paced.

Words like "however," "moreover," "consequently," "then," "therefore," "nevertheless," are often used to connect two main clauses. When they do, they should be preceded by a semicolon. "Tomorrow is a holiday; consequently, the banks will be closed." "The police arrested the informer; however, he refused to assist them in their investigation." Be careful of these words, however, when they are not joining main clauses. Then they usually are set off by commas. "Women painters, however, have always comprised a small minority."

Occasionally, a semicolon replaces the comma before "and," "or," "but," "nor," "for," when these words are used to join two sentences (main clauses). The semicolon is preferred when the clauses are long or contain coordinate elements. In such cases, the value of the semicolon is that it demands more attention than the comma. It emphasizes the distinction between clauses. "We had gone down the road originally to look at a house set in the woods, with gingerbread trim, a red roof, and seven chimneys; but when we got there, we found it had been so damaged by vandals that we could not hope to restore it."

Be careful about substituting a semicolon for a comma when two clauses are not involved. You can never use a semicolon to set off a clause and a phrase. Never write: "I have always enjoyed collecting antiques; especially early American furniture." Never write: "She sat on a straight-backed wooden chair in the anteroom; nervously awaiting the appearance of the doctor.

The dash is also a useful mark of punctuation. Writers unfamiliar with it tend to avoid it or to use it far too often. It has specific uses and should not be used simply because you are not sure what other punctuation mark is correct. The hallmark of the dash is informality. It has two distinct uses.

A single dash operates as an informal colon. "He was extremely good at one thing—repairing cars." "Air travel has two selling points—speed and comfort."

Two dashes work as an informal set of parentheses. "Did you see my friend—Alvin, not James—on stage?" "She did not take her raincoat—although I had asked her to—when she went to the store."

Most typewriters do not have a dash on the keyboard. The commonly accepted substitute is *two* hyphens. If the writing is to be published, the two hyphens signal the typesetter that a dash is wanted.

One hundred commonly misspelled words

accede	commitment	familiar
accommodate	concede	feasible
accumulate	conscience	fluorescent
acknowledgment	conscious	foreign
acquaintance	convenience	forty
acquire	criticize	government
acquittal	deceive	grammar
affect (to	defendant	grievous,
influence)	definite	grudge
all right	description	height
appearance	dissatisfied	hindrance
argument	ecstasy	hypocrisy
attendance	effect (result)	idiosyncrasy
behavior	embarrass	independence
beneficial	eminent	interfere
calendar	envelop (verb)	irresistible
canvass (verb)	exaggerate	judgment
cemetery	exhibition	kerosene
chauffeur	existence	kidnaped - *kidnapped* ?

lacquer
ledger
legitimate
leisure
license
lightning
liquefy
maintenance
manageable
maneuver
mileage
miscellaneous
mortgage
noticeable
nuisance

occasion
occurrence
optimism
pageant
pamphlet
parallel
peculiar
plagiarism
possession
precede
prejudice
privilege
probably
publicly
reconcile

recurrence
restaurant
rhyme
ridiculous
sensible
separate
similar
specifically
stationary (fixed)
stationery (paper)
temperament
unkempt
vaccinate
vegetable

Suggestions
for Further Reading

BARNET, SYLVAN, and MARCIA STUBBS, *Barnet and Stubbs's Practical Guide to Writing* (rev. ed.). Boston: Little Brown and Company, 1977.

BATES, JEFFERSON D., *Writing With Precision: How to Write So That You Cannot Possibly Be Misunderstood* (2nd ed.). Washington, D.C.: Acropolis Books Ltd., 1978.

BARZUN, JACQUES, and HENRY F. GRAFF, *The Modern Researcher* (3rd ed.), pp. 209–261. New York: Harcourt Brace Jovanovich, Inc., 1977.

BERNSTEIN, THEODORE M., *The Careful Writer: A Modern Guide to English Usage.* New York: Atheneum, 1977.

GORREL, L. ROBERT, and CHARLTON LAIRD, *Modern English Handbook* (6th ed.). Englewood Cliffs, N.J.: Prentice-Hall, Inc., 1976.

HALL, DONALD, *Writing Well* (3rd ed.). Boston: Little Brown and Company, 1979.

HODGES, JOHN C., and MARY E. WHITTEN, *Harbrace College Handbook* (8th ed.). New York: Harcourt Brace Jovanovich, Inc., 1977.

LEFCOWITZ, ALLAN B., *The Writer's Handbook.* Englewood Cliffs, N.J.: Prentice-Hall, Inc., 1976.

MCCRIMMON, JAMES, *Writing With a Purpose* (6th ed.). Boston: Houghton Mifflin Company, 1976.

MINOT, STEPHEN, *Three Genres: The Writing of Poetry, Fiction and Drama* (2nd ed.). Englewood Cliffs, N.J.: Prentice-Hall, Inc., 1971.

The New York Times Manual of Style and Usage: A Desk Book of Guidelines for Writers and Editors, ed. Lewis Jordan. New York: Quadrangle/The New York Times Book Company, 1976.

OSTROM, JOHN, *Better Paragraphs* (4th ed.). New York: Chandler Publishing Company, 1978.

RIVERS, WILLIAM L., *Writing: Craft and Art.* Englewood Cliffs, N.J.: Prentice-Hall, Inc., 1975.

STRUNK, WILLIAM, JR., and E. B. WHITE, *The Elements of Style* (3rd ed.). New York: Macmillan Publishing Co., Inc., 1979.

TRIMBLE, JOHN R., *Writing With Style: Conversations on the Art of Writing.* Englewood Cliffs, N.J.: Prentice-Hall, Inc., 1975.

WALPOLE, JANE R., *A Writer's Guide: Easy Ground Rules for Successful Written English.* Englewood Cliffs, N.J.: Prentice-Hall, Inc., 1980.

ZINSSER, WILLIAM, *On Writing Well: An Informal Guide to Writing Nonfiction* (2nd ed.). New York: Harper & Row, 1980.

Index

159